Name _____

**Read the story.**

Let's learn how to mix paint. You can make a new color. Get a small dish. Put some yellow paint in the dish. Add a little bit of blue paint. Now stir to mix the new color. You made green paint.

**Read the sentences in the box below. Write them in order as they happened in the story.**

**1** _____

**2** _____

**3** _____

**4** _____

**5** _____

| Put the yellow paint in the dish. |
|---|
| Stir the paint. |
| Look at the green paint. |
| Get a dish. |
| Add some blue paint. |

**Draw a line under the best ending for the story.**

You can eat lunch.
You can paint a tree.
You have three new colors.

FS-32044 Reading

Name _____

**Read the story.**

Every morning I must get ready for school. I do not want to miss the bus. After breakfast I put my books in my book bag. Then I put on my coat and walk to the bus stop. I wait for the bus with my friends. The bus comes at eight o'clock.

**Read the sentences in the box below. Write them in order as they happened in the story.**

**1**
_____

**2**
_____

**3**
_____

**4**
_____

**5**
_____

| I go to the bus stop. |
| I put my books in my bag. |
| I eat breakfast. |
| I put on my coat. |
| I wait for the bus. |

**Draw a line under the best ending for the story.**

I will walk to school.

I ride the bus to the store.

I ride the bus to school.

2

Name _____

**Read the story.**

Dad and I went to the park. We were going to rent a boat for an hour. Dad paid for the boat. I got into the boat. Dad climbed in. We rowed around the pond. I learned to steer and row the boat.

**Read the sentences in the box below. Write them in order as they happened in the story.**

**1** _____

**2** _____

**3** _____

**4** _____

**5** _____

| |
|---|
| I climbed into the boat. |
| We rowed around the pond. |
| Dad paid for the boat. |
| Dad got in the boat. |
| We went to the park. |

**Draw a line under the best ending for the story.**

We rowed out to the ocean.

We took the boat back to the dock.

We took the boat home.

Name _____

**Read the story.**

Tomorrow is my friend's birthday party. I bought a book for her. I put a picture of myself inside the book cover. I put the book in a box. I wrapped the box in pink and yellow paper. I wrote, "Happy Birthday to Jan—from Kim".

**Read the sentences in the box below. Write them in order as they happened in the story.**

**1** _____

**2** _____

**3** _____

**4** _____

**5** _____

| I bought a book. |
| I wrapped the gift. |
| I put it in a box. |
| I wrote a note. |
| I put my picture in the book. |

**Draw a line under the best ending for the story.**

Kim keeps the book.
Kim mails the gift to Jim
Kim goes to Jan's party.

4

FS-32044 Reading

Name _____

**Read the story.**

    I need to talk to Ted. I looked up his telephone number and called his house. His mother said, "Call back after five o'clock." I will call Ted again just before dinner. He will be home then.

**Read the sentences in the box below. Write them in order as they happened in the story.**

**1** _____

**2** _____

**3** _____

**4** _____

**5** _____

| |
|---|
| She said, "Ted is not home." |
| I looked up Ted's number. |
| I talked to his mother. |
| I called his house. |
| She asked me to call later. |

**Draw a line under the best ending for the story.**

Ted will call me.

I talk to Jack on the telephone.

I will call again and talk to Ted.

FS-32044 Reading

Name _____

**Read the story.**

Meg was on the swing. She said, "Watch me!" She jumped off while she was still swinging. Meg fell down and hurt her leg. She cried. She walked to the office. Meg told the nurse about her leg.

**Read the sentences in the box below. Write them in order as they happened in the story.**

**1** _____

**2** _____

**3** _____

**4** _____

**5** _____

| Meg jumped from the swing. |
| Meg was swinging. |
| Meg cried. |
| Meg walked to the office. |
| Meg said, "Watch me!" |

**Draw a line under the best ending for the story.**

Meg said, "This is fun."
The school nurse will help Meg.
Meg lost her shoe.

6

Name _____

**Read the story.**

My grandmother gave me a new game. I asked my sister to play the game with me. The doorbell rang. It was my friend Don. He played the game with us. Mother wants to play the game after dinner. That will be fun!

**Read the sentences in the box below. Write them in order as they happened in the story.**

**1** _____

**2** _____

**3** _____

**4** _____

**5** _____

| Don played with us. |
| I asked my sister to play. |
| Mother wants to play later. |
| I have a new game. |
| Someone was at the door. |

**Draw a line under the best ending for the story.**

Mother can't find the game.
Don took the game home.
I wrote a thank you note to Grandmother.

     FS-32044 Reading

Name _____

**Read the story.**

The traffic light is broken. A policewoman is telling the cars when to go. Two men came in a yellow truck to fix the light. Their truck had a ladder on it. One man climbed up and fixed the light. The policewoman and workmen left.

**Read the sentences in the box below. Write them in order as they happened in the story.**

**1**
_____

**2**
_____

**3**
_____

**4**
_____

**5**
_____

| The workmen fixed the light. |
| A yellow truck came. |
| She told the cars when to go. |
| Two men worked on the light. |
| The workmen went away. |

**Draw a line under the best ending for the story.**

Now the light is working fine.
They took the light down.
They put in a stop sign.

8

FS-32044 Reading

Name _____

**Read the story.**

    On Saturdays Dad and I clean up our yard. I rake the leaves. Dad pulls the weeds while I cut the grass. Then we sweep the sidewalk. We water the plants if it has not rained during the week. If it rains on Saturday and Sunday we do not do yard work.

**Read the sentences in the box below. Write them in order as they happened in the story.**

**1** _____

**2** _____

**3** _____

**4** _____

**5** _____

| We water the plants. |
| Dad and I go outside. |
| I rake the leaves. |
| I cut the grass. |
| We sweep the sidewalk. |

**Draw a line under the best ending for the story.**

Dad digs a big hole in the grass.

Mother says, "The yard looks nice."

Mother says, "Our yard looks dirty."

9

Name _____

**Read the story.**

I wanted a pet bird so I bought a cage. I saved money to buy the bird. Before school I give him food and water. I put clean paper on the bottom of the cage. Before I go to bed I cover his cage with a blanket. Then he is warm at night.

**Read the sentences in the box below. Write them in order as they happened in the story.**

**1** _____

**2** _____

**3** _____

**4** _____

**5** _____

| |
|---|
| I feed my bird. |
| I bought a bird. |
| I put paper in his cage. |
| I bought a cage. |
| I put a blanket over the cage. |

**Draw a line under the best ending for the story.**

The bird flies to the top of the tree.
The bird goes to sleep.
The bird is my brother's pet.

FS-32044 Reading

Name _____

**Read the story.**

I must unlock my bike and I can't find the key anywhere. Will you help me? It is a silver key. Please look in my room. I'll go ask my mother if she has seen it. It may be in the pocket of my other pants.

**Read the sentences in the box below. Write them in order as they happened in the story.**

**1** _____

**2** _____

**3** _____

**4** _____

**5** _____

| |
|---|
| I must unlock my bike. |
| I will ask Mother. |
| Look for the key in my room. |
| Maybe it's in my other pants. |
| My key is lost. |

**Draw a line under the best ending for the story.**

I found the key in my pants pocket.

I found the missing bike.

I do not need a key.

 FS-32044 Reading

**Read the story.**

Tom is getting ready for a camping trip. His flashlight will not work. The light bulb is broken. At the store he found the bulb he needed. He bought the bulb and put it in. Now the flashlight works again.

**Read the sentences in the box below. Write them in order as they happened in the story.**

1 _____

2 _____

3 _____

4 _____

5 _____

| |
|---|
| The flashlight needs a bulb. |
| Now the flashlight works. |
| He put in the light bulb. |
| Tom went to the store. |
| He found the bulb. |

**Draw a line under the best ending for the story.**

The flashlight will not work.

Tom hides the flashlight.

Tom takes the flashlight with him.

Name _____

**Read the story.**

Our neighbors are away on vacation. Mr. Jones asked me to take care of their home. I must feed their cat. I pick up the mail. After school I get the paper from the driveway. They will pay me for taking good care of their home.

**Read the sentences in the box below. Write them in order as they happened in the story.**

1 _____

2 _____

3 _____

4 _____

5 _____

| I feed the cat. |
| I take care of the mail. |
| Mr. Jones asked me to help. |
| I will be paid. |
| I pick up the paper. |

**Draw a line under the best ending for the story.**

Mr. Jones is angry.

Mr. Jones pays me for doing a good job.

Mr. Jones does not care about his house.

Name _____

**Read the story.**

We have a special reading time at school. Everyone picks a book to read. I have my own quiet reading time at home now. At bedtime I get ready and then I look at the clock. I read for fifteen minutes. Then I turn out the light. My reading time at home adds up to 105 minutes each week.

**Read the sentences in the box below. Write them in order as they happened in the story.**

**1**
_____

**2**
_____

**3**
_____

**4**
_____

**5**
_____

| |
|---|
| I get ready for bed. |
| We have reading at school. |
| I have reading time at home. |
| I turn out the light. |
| I read for fifteen minutes. |

**Draw a line under the best ending for the story.**

I cannot find my book.

I read many books.

I do not have a library card.

Name _____

**Read the story.**

    My dance class is on Thursdays. I bring my tap shoes to school. I go to dance class on the bus after school. I put on my tap shoes. Then I take my lesson. After class my brother takes me home.

**Read the sentences in the box below. Write them in order as they happened in the story.**

**1** _____

**2** _____

**3** _____

**4** _____

**5** _____

| I ride the bus to dancing school. |
| I put on my tap shoes. |
| I take my dancing shoes to school. |
| My brother takes me home. |
| My dancing lesson begins. |

**Draw a line under the best ending for the story.**

I practice tap dancing at home.

I only dance on Thursdays.

I must get new shoes.

Name _____

**Read the story.**

    I started a club. I asked a few friends to join. Five of my friends said yes. We had our first club meeting. We have a name for our club—THE SUPER KIDS. We will have a campout in Jim's yard.

**Read the sentences in the box below. Write them in order as they happened in the story.**

**1** _____

**2** _____

**3** _____

**4** _____

**5** _____

| We had our first meeting. |
| Five people joined my club. |
| I asked some friends to join. |
| We plan to have a campout. |
| I wanted to start a club. |

**Draw a line under the best ending for the story.**

It is hard to start a club.
It costs too much money to have a club.
The campout is fun for everyone.

                      FS-32044 Reading

**Read the story.**

I made a book about football. On the cover I wrote the names of football players. I found pictures and stories about football. I cut them out and pasted them in my book. On Friday it will be my turn to share at school. I will share my football book.

**Read the sentences in the box below. Write them in order as they happened in the story.**

**1** _____

**2** _____

**3** _____

**4** _____

**5** _____

| |
|---|
| I wrote names on the cover. |
| I made a book. |
| I cut out pictures and stories. |
| I will take it to school. |
| I pasted pictures in my book. |

**Draw a line under the best ending for the story.**

I do not show the book to anyone.
I show the book to my class on Friday.
I took the book back to the library.

Name _____

**Read the story.**

    My brother is having a birthday party. His friends will come. They will play lots of games. Mom made a big cake. We set the table. We have party hats for everyone. Dad and I blew up balloons. We are ready to begin.

**Read the sentences in the box below. Write them in order as they happened in the story.**

**1** _____

**2** _____

**3** _____

**4** _____

**5** _____

| A big cake is made. |
| We blew up balloons. |
| There is going to be a party. |
| Everything is ready. |
| Everyone will have a hat. |

**Draw a line under the best ending for the story.**

We must buy a cake.
The Christmas party is fun.
The doorbell rings and everyone comes in.

Name _____

**Read the story.**

Let's go fishing. Put a piece of bait on the hook. Throw your line in the water. Watch the float. When it moves up and down a fish is eating the bait. Pull up the rod and wind it in. Maybe you will have a fish.

**Read the sentences in the box below. Write them in order as they happened in the story.**

**1** _____

**2** _____

**3** _____

**4** _____

**5** _____

| First you must bait your hook. |
| Put the line in the water. |
| Let's go fishing. |
| Watch the float carefully. |
| Pull in the fish. |

**Draw a line under the best ending for the story.**

You can eat the fish for dinner.
There are no fish in the lake.
I am afraid of turtles.

FS-32044 Reading

Name _____

**Read the story.**

Our shoe store is having a sale. Dad and I went to the store. I tried on a pair of blue shoes. They were too small. I tried on some brown shoes. I wanted blue in a bigger size. We bought bigger blue shoes.

**Read the sentences in the box below. Write them in order as they happened in the story.**

**1** _____

**2** _____

**3** _____

**4** _____

**5** _____

| We went to the shoe store. |
| Shoes are on sale. |
| I tried on small shoes. |
| I bought blue shoes. |
| I tried on brown shoes. |

**Draw a line under the best ending for the story.**

I wore the blue shoes to school.
Dad wore the new shoes to work.
We bought two pairs of shoes.

FS-32044 Reading

**Name** _____

Dear Donna,

I would like you to come to a party at my house next Saturday. It is going to be a surprise birthday party for Judy.

We are going to have hot dogs and chips for lunch. My mother has bought some new games for us to play. Then we will light seven candles on the cake for Judy to blow out. We'll have ice cream to eat too, and something cold to drink. At 3 o'clock my mother is going to take us to the show to see "Cricket Goes to Washington". I hope you can come.

Be sure to be here before 12 o'clock.

Love,
Molly

1. **A good name for this story would be:**

   a. Going to the Show
   b. A Surprise Party
   c. Eating Cake and Ice Cream

2. **Molly is writing a _____ to Donna.**

   a. test
   b. letter
   c. paper

3. **Who is going to be seven years old?**

   a. Molly
   b. Nancy
   c. Judy

4. **What word in the story means "to wish"?**

   a. hope
   b. lost
   c. eat

5. **How do you think Judy will feel when she comes to Molly's house?**

   a. happy
   b. sad
   c. angry

RATCHETY RATCH

"I am a blue bird. Green trees are nice and red flowers are pretty, but I think they would look better if they were blue like me. I'll ask Homer if I can use some of his blue paint tonight."

"Help yourself, Blue Bird," Homer said, hopping around his cage. "But be sure to bring it back. I have to paint my Easter eggs soon."

Blue Bird flew from tree to tree painting everything blue. The next morning all the neighbors came outside. "What has happened? All the colors are gone! Blue is such a sad color." And they all began to cry.

"I guess not everyone likes blue the best. I'll wash all the trees and flowers tonight and then they will all be happy again."

1. **A good name for this story would be:**

   a. A Bird That Likes Blue
   b. Painting at Night
   c. Coloring Trees and Flowers

2. **Homer wanted Blue Bird to _____ his paints.**

   a. throw away
   b. drink
   c. return

3. **Where did Blue Bird do most of his painting?**

   a. under the houses
   b. in the gardens
   c. in Homer's cage

4. **What word in the story means "unhappy"?**

   a. best
   b. sad
   c. soon

5. **Homer has to paint his eggs soon. What do you think Homer is?**

   a. a dog
   b. a rabbit
   c. a chicken

       FS-32044 Reading

The mother hen sat on her eggs all night. Early the next morning, one egg popped open and out jumped a mouse. "What are you doing here? You're not one of my babies!" cried the hen.

"I don't have a mother to take care of me," the little mouse answered. "But if you will help me, I can look like one of your babies." One by one, the mouse brought some feathers to the mother hen. "Stick these on my back. Now, don't I look soft and furry?"

Just then, a little chicken walked over. "Do you want to go out and play with me?"

"Squeak, squeak, squeak," the mouse said.

"Oh, no," sighed the mother hen. "Now what do I do with you?"

1. **A good name for this story would be:**

   a. Mother Hen's New Baby
   b. **A Duck Goes Out to Play**
   c. **Animals in the Barn**

2. **"I don't have a mother. Can I be your**
   **_____ ?"**

   a. chicken
   b. baby
   c. mouse

3. **When did mother hen sit on her eggs?**

   a. in the morning
   b. at night
   c. before lunch

4. **What word in the story means the opposite of "late"?**

   _____

5. **What do you think the mother hen will do next?**

   a. teach the mouse to quack
   b. teach the mouse to meow
   c. teach the mouse to cluck

It was a very hot summer day. "I need to cool off," Barbie thought to herself, walking through an empty lot. Right in the middle of the lot, she saw a bush and sat under it.

"Ouch! You are sitting on my foot, little girl."

Barbie jumped up in surprise. "What are you?" she asked.

"A Wafflelumper."

Barbie couldn't believe what she was seeing. "And where are you from?"

"The North Pole. I didn't know it was going to be so hot here. You see, if I don't stay under this bush where it is cool, my feet will turn from waffles into pancakes. Then I would not be able to stand up on the ice. I hope winter comes pretty soon so I can start walking home again."

1. **A good name for this story would be:**
   a. **Barbie Meets a Wafflelumper**
   b. A Hot Summer Day
   c. Cooling Off Under a Bush

2. **Barbie found a place in the _____ to cool off.**
   a. sun
   b. shade
   c. house

HI! I'M WALLY THE WAFFLELUMPER!

3. **Where did Barbie sit on the Wafflelumper?**
   a. in the lot
   b. under a bush
   c. at the North Pole

4. **What word in the story means "not hot"?**
   a. empty
   b. cool
   c. winter

5. **You can tell Barbie had**
   a. never been in an empty lot.
   b. never seen a Wafflelumper.
   c. never been to the North Pole.

**Name** _____

Adam hopped out of bed early Sunday morning just as the sun was coming up. "I hope the Easter Bunny left me lots of eggs and some candy." He looked all around. He hunted and hunted but couldn't find one egg. When he looked behind the last big bush in his yard, Adam saw something that made his hair stand on end.

"What are you doing here, Santa Claus? This is Easter, not Christmas!"

"The Easter Bunny is sick today and he gave me this basket to take around to all the houses. But he didn't tell me where to leave these eggs."

"I'll show you what to do, Santa Claus." They hopped off down the street, hiding eggs in the grass and under the flowers.

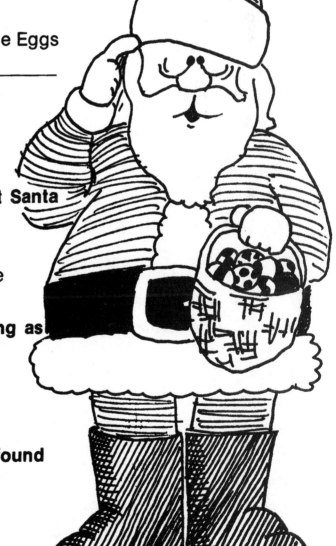

1. **A good name for this story would be:**

   a. A Christmas Story
   b. Santa Claus Finds a Helper
   c. The Easter Bunny Brings Some Eggs

2. **Adam looked all around his _____ for eggs.**

   a. house
   b. garden
   c. room

3. **What did the Easter Bunny want Santa Claus to do?**

   a. hide the eggs and candy
   b. wait for him at Adam's house
   c. color all the eggs yellow

4. **What word means the same thing as "looked for"?**

   a. left
   b. hopped
   c. hunted

5. **Santa Claus felt glad when he found someone to**

   a. help him.
   b. feed him.
   c. talk to him.

"Michelle, why are you still awake?" Mother asked, sitting on the bed. "It's after 10 o'clock."

"I'm waiting for the airplane. After I go to sleep tonight, I thought I might like to take a trip to Terry's house. I read about her in a book today. She lives far away in a place called Hawaii. Every day Terry and her friends go swimming, take a boat ride and play in the sand. Then maybe someday, when Terry is sound asleep, she can fly over here to our house and I'll show her how to build a snowman."

"I hope you have a good time tonight, Michelle," Mother said, "but be sure to be back at 7 in the morning so you will get to school on time."

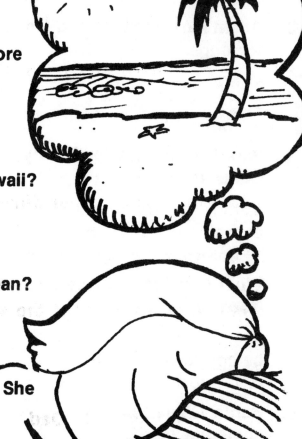

1. **A good name for this story would be:**

   a. Playing by the Sea
   b. Going to School
   c. Dreaming About a Trip

2. **Michelle had to fall _____ before taking a trip.**

   a. down
   b. awake
   c. asleep

3. **What was Michelle going to do in Hawaii?**

   a. work and read
   b. swim and play
   c. write and ride

4. **Which word reminds you of the ocean?**

   a. ride
   b. sand
   c. school

5. **Michelle did not really go to Hawaii. She was only**

   a. thinking.
   b. dreaming.
   c. playing.

My mother left town this morning to go and visit my grandfather and she won't be back for two days. Tonight my Dad fixed dinner for my sister and me. He stayed in the kitchen for a long time. I thought he was making enough food to last for both days. When Dad called us to the table, I was a little surprised. It looked very different from what mother cooks for dinner. Here is what we had:

    4 pieces of bread (a little burned), peanut butter (no jelly), spaghetti (with hot dogs on top), popcorn (no butter)

"This looks really good!" Marla said. "Don't you think so, Jeff? I sure hope Mom stays at grandfather's for two or three weeks so you can cook for us all the time, Dad."

**1. A good name for this story would be:**

  a. Dad Takes Over in the Kitchen
  b. Mother Goes to Grandfather's
  c. Dad Burns the Dinner

**2. Marla wanted Dad to fix dinner _____ .**

  a. one night
  b. every night
  c. in the morning

**3. What did Dad cook for dinner?**

  a. eggs
  b. bananas
  c. popcorn

**4. What word means "not the same"?**

  a. burned
  b. different
  c. enough

**5. You might think that Dad**

  a. was too tired to cook.
  b. had never cooked dinner before.
  c. did not like meat.

"Who spilled this milk all over the kitchen floor?" Mother shouted. "Do you know who did this, Marty?"

"My hand did it. I told it to be careful, but it went ahead and dropped the bottle anyway. That was my right hand. This morning, my left hand broke your best dish in the backyard. The pieces flew everywhere! While I was cleaning up the dish, both of my feet stepped into your flower garden. I said, 'Watch out, feet!' but it was too late. There are no flowers anymore."

"I think I better take you to the doctor and have him give you some new hands and feet," Mother said.

"Wait a minute, Mother. From now on, I'll tell my hands and feet to be careful and stay out of trouble."

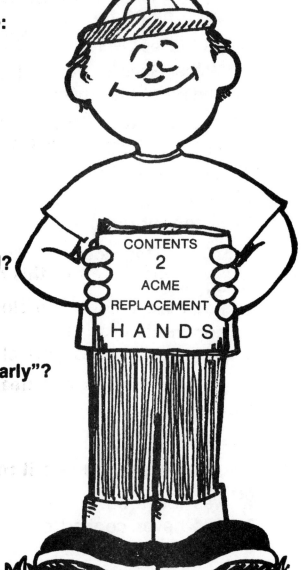

1. **A good name for this story would be:**

   a. Hands and Feet in Trouble
   b. Cleaning Up the House
   c. Going to the Doctor

2. **Marty _____ to his feet in the garden.**

   a. barked
   b. quacked
   c. talked

3. **What did Marty drop with his right hand?**

   a. flowers
   b. milk
   c. pieces

4. **What word in the story means "not early"?**

   a. broke
   b. minute
   c. late

5. **Marty's hands and feet would not**

   a. clean up the floor.
   b. do what he told them to.
   c. go to the store.

28

I have a face, but no mouth, no eyes and no nose. I have two **hands** and sometimes even three. You need me to tell you when to go to bed and when to get up. I sometimes make a loud buzzing sound to wake you up at dawn.

You can hang me on the wall or put me on the table. If I am very big, people call me "grandfather". One time, a mouse ran up me and then back down again. I cannot talk, but I can tick.

Can you tell me what I am?

1. **A good name for this story would be:**

   a. Time to Get Up
   b. Guess What I Am?
   c. Learning to Tell Time

2. **If you don't have a clock, a _____ can tell the time.**

   a. watch
   b. record
   c. dancer

3. **What do the <u>hands</u> in this story do?**

   a. clean the face of the clock
   b. tell the time of day
   c. point to letters on the clock

4. **What word in the story means "early in morning"?**

   _____

5. **If a clock says 6 o'clock, it could be time for**

   a. dinner.
   b. school.
   c. lunch.

FS-32044 Reading

"I wish I could be someone's pet, but nobody seems to want a rat around the house. Maybe if I went down to the pet shop, Mr. Sam would put me in his window where all the children would notice me. This weekend, I'll learn how to roll over like a dog, purr like a cat and sing like a bird."

Monday morning, the little rat skipped over to the pet store, bounced up on Mr. Sam's lap and meowed as soft as he could.

"You can't fool me," said Mr. Sam. "I know a rat when I see one. Don't be sad because you can't be a pet. We need good rats like you to eat up all the bad spiders and bugs in the city that might hurt people. If you work hard, I'll write a story about you in the Animal Book called: 'OUR HERO, THE RAT.'"

1. **The <u>best</u> name for this story would be:**
   a. A Sad Rat
   b. A Rat Wants to Be a Pet
   c. A Rat That Learns to Purr

2. **Mr. Sam owned a store with many _____ in it.**
   a. elephants
   b. animals
   c. zebras

3. **When did the rat learn to purr and sing?**
   a. on Monday
   b. on the weekend
   c. on the last day

4. **What word in the story means "a brave and strong person"?**

   _____

5. **What should the rat do now?**
   a. stay at Mr. Sam's pet shop
   b. catch insects that harm people
   c. eat lady bugs and snails

 FS-32044 Reading

"I'm going to build my own house right here in this tree. It will be just for my friends and me. We can eat cookies and drink milk up here."

"That sounds like a good idea," Mother told Millie. "I'll get you a **saw** and some wood and nails to use when you are building your house."

Millie climbed up the tree and worked very hard all afternoon. She sawed **away** some branches to make room for the kitchen and a window too. Soon she was all finished.

"Mother, I can't get down," Millie shouted. "I cut off too many branches and now I'm stuck up here in this tree."

1. **The best name for this story would be:**
   a. Millie Builds a Tree House
   b. Building With Nails and Wood
   c. A Tree House for Friends

2. **Millie will need to get a _____ to get down.**
   a. chair
   b. ladder
   c. swing

3. **Millie needed three things to build with:**
   a. a saw, nails and branches
   b. a tree, wood and nails
   c. a saw, wood and nails

4. **The word saw in this story means:**
   a. to see someone
   b. a tool to cut with
   c. something to climb on

5. **You can tell that Millie did not**
   a. want to build a tree house.
   b. plan ahead before sawing.
   c. know how to climb a tree.

I look just like my brother and he looks very much like me. My mother gets mixed up sometimes and calls me John instead of Jim. I don't mind, though, except when John gets into trouble and I get sent to my room by mistake. We can share our clothes and shoes because we are both the same size and shape.

Most people can't tell us apart. We like to fool the teacher by answering questions at the same time and changing chairs when she is not looking. All our friends call us John-Jim and Jim-John. They can never tell which is which. John and I have a secret that no one has discovered yet.

John can whistle, but I can't!

HE'S JOHN!

1. **The <u>best</u> name for this story would be:**

   a. Look-Alike Brothers
   b. Jim Can't Whistle
   c. Two Brothers in Trouble

2. **John and Jim can wear each other's**
   _____ .

   a. teeth
   b. shirts
   c. radios

3. **What can John do that Jim can't do?**

   a. get in trouble
   b. wear his pants
   c. whistle a tune

4. **What word in the story means the opposite of "always"?**

   _____

5. **The story does not say, but you can tell John and Jim are:**

   a. good friends
   b. twin brothers
   c. older and younger

Father stood in the doorway and watched Toby pack his clothes in a bag. "Where are you going, Toby?"

"I'm leaving home, Dad. I'm taking my bike and riding far away. I'm kind of tired of cleaning my room and washing dishes. I just want to ride and play from now on."

"I'm sorry you will have to leave so soon. Who will go to the ocean with me this summer?" asked Father. "What will I do with this new kite I bought? I guess I'll just have to get myself another son."

Toby sat down and thought a minute. "Maybe I could stay for one more day if you need someone to help you fly that kite."

1. **A good name for this story would be:**

    a. Riding Bikes and Having Fun
    b. A Run-Away Stays Home
    c. Leaving Home With Father

2. **Toby would probably not like to _____ clothes.**

    a. wear
    b. wash
    c. buy

3. **When did Dad plan to go to the ocean?**

    a. in July
    b. during Easter
    c. when it rained

4. **What word in the story means the opposite of "later"?**

5. **What can you tell about Toby?**

    a. He didn't really want to leave home.
    b. He didn't know how to pack his clothes.
    c. He didn't know where to run away to.

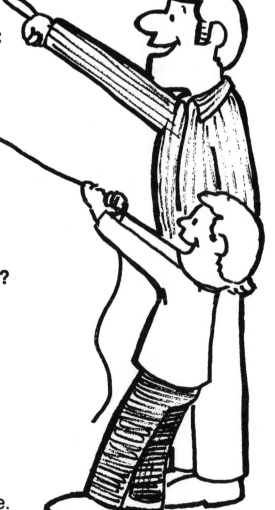

 FS-32044 Reading

"Eat your carrots, Debbie," Mother said leaving the kitchen. "Vegetables are good for you. Remember, no ice cream until you finish."

"Blah! I could get sick if I eat these." Just as Debbie was about to take her first bite, she felt a tail rub against her leg. "Rufus! You're just in time," she whispered. "Have a carrot." Debbie fed her dog four more carrots and then told him to go out the back door. "All finished, Mom. Come look."

"Open your mouth, Debbie. I want to see if you are hiding any in there." Debbie opened wide. "Debbie Teasdale, what have you done with those carrots? If you really ate your carrots, your teeth would be orange, but yours are as white as can be!"

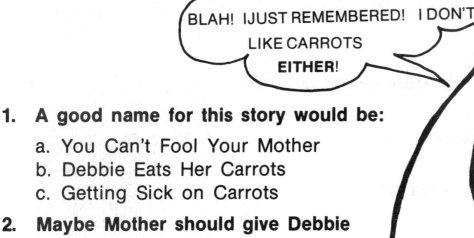

1. **A good name for this story would be:**

   a. You Can't Fool Your Mother
   b. Debbie Eats Her Carrots
   c. Getting Sick on Carrots

2. **Maybe Mother should give Debbie**

   a. some ice cream.
   b. a new dog.
   c. a different vegetable.

3. **Where was Rufus eating the carrots?**

   a. in the backyard
   b. under the table
   c. in the closet

4. **What word in the story names a "part of the face"?**

   _____

5. **What will happen to Debbie now?**

   a. She will have to go to bed.
   b. Mother will give her some bread.
   c. She cannot have anything to eat after dinner.

34

**Name** _____

While walking home one evening by moonlight, I had the feeling someone was following me. I stopped a minute to listen and then said to myself, "You had better start running, Tommy, before he catches up to you." I squeezed under a fence and took a shortcut through Mr. Gumper's backyard. But I knew he was still there, only a few feet away.

I raced home as fast as I could and locked the front door. As soon as I turned on the light, there he was again, standing by the wall.

When I woke up the next morning, there wasn't a sign of my follower anywhere, although I know he will be back again tonight to follow me around by the moonlight. I'm not afraid because he has been walking behind me for almost nine years. We are good friends, my shadow and me.

1. **The best name for this story would be:**
   a. My Shadow and Me
   b. Walking Home at Night
   c. My Best Friend

2. **Most of the time shadows are**

   _____ .

   a. yellow
   b. dark
   c. round

3. **Where did the shadow follow Tommy?**
   a. through the woods
   b. to the store
   c. under a fence

4. **What word in the story means to "stay behind someone"?**

   _____

5. **The story doesn't say so but Tommy's shadow did not:**
   a. follow him
   b. like him
   c. scare him

Once, many years ago, a fire destroyed most of a large forest. The animals had no homes. Forest rangers found many young animals, including a small bear who was clinging to a half-burned tree. He was quite scared! They **rescued** the little cub and decided to name him Smokey.

Today Smokey is famous. You may see his picture on posters and T.V. ads. He reminds us to prevent forest fires.

1. **The best title for this story is:**
   a. Smokey the Bear
   b. Forest Fires
   c. Preventing Forest Fires
   d. Life In the Forest

2. **The little bear was found:**
   a. during the fire
   b. clinging to a tree
   c. by a small child
   d. by the roadside

3. **While the forest was burning the little animal was:**
   a. happy
   b. tired
   c. frightened
   d. mad

4. **Smokey is famous because:**
   a. he fights fires
   b. he protects the forest
   c. his picture reminds us to prevent fires
   d. he is a cute bear

5. **In the story, the word "rescued" means:**
   a. ran away
   b. saved
   c. held
   d. found

6. **If this particular bear cub had not been found:**
   a. people would not prevent forest fires
   b. we would use a deer instead of Smokey
   c. we would not use Smokey
   d. both A and B

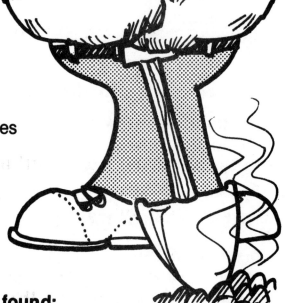

Making potato prints is a lot of fun. First you cut a potato in half. Draw a design on one of the **flat** halves. Cut away the potato around the design. A small knife would be the best tool. Put poster paint on the design with a brush. Print it on paper.

1.  **The best title for this story is:**
    a.  Cutting Potatos
    b.  Painting Designs
    c.  Potato Prints
    d.  The Tools

2.  **The story tells you to put paint on:**
    a.  the paper
    b.  the design
    c.  the dish
    d.  the tool

3.  **A good tool to use:**
    a.  a spoon
    b.  a knife
    c.  a nail
    d.  your scissors

4.  **The best way to put paint on is:**
    a.  to dip the potato
    b.  with your finger
    c.  with a brush
    d.  pour it on gently

5.  **In the story, the word "flat" means:**
    a.  a dull color
    b.  an apartment
    c.  level
    d.  not on key

6.  **Another article most like this one would be:**
    a.  Vacations
    b.  Art in America
    c.  Block Printing Fun
    d.  Potato Pancakes

One day Fluffy ran across the **yard**. She saw some birds flying from branch to branch in the old maple tree. Without thinking, Fluffy climbed the tree. The birds flew away. Fluffy tried to get down but she didn't know how. Mrs. Jones tried to help, but she couldn't reach her cat. She decided to call the Fire Department for help.

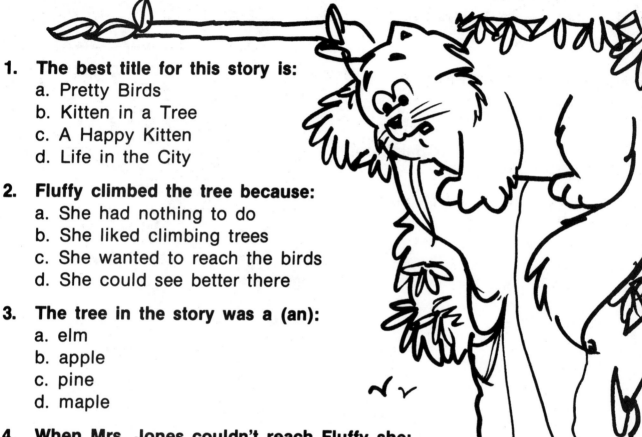

1. **The best title for this story is:**
   a. Pretty Birds
   b. Kitten in a Tree
   c. A Happy Kitten
   d. Life in the City

2. **Fluffy climbed the tree because:**
   a. She had nothing to do
   b. She liked climbing trees
   c. She wanted to reach the birds
   d. She could see better there

3. **The tree in the story was a (an):**
   a. elm
   b. apple
   c. pine
   d. maple

4. **When Mrs. Jones couldn't reach Fluffy she:**
   a. decided to call for help
   b. got a ladder
   c. called Fluffy to come down
   d. asked a neighbor for help

5. **In the story, the word "yard" means:**
   a. a measure
   b. three feet
   c. a piece of cloth
   d. a piece of ground

6. **The story probably ended when:**
   a. Mrs. Jones climbed the tree
   b. Fluffy climbed down
   c. the Fire Department came and helped
   d. it rained

FS-32044 Reading

In the **fall**, leaves drop to the ground. Animals may begin to store food. Days become shorter. Cold weather is coming and many birds fly south. People wear warmer clothing and prepare for winter. In some areas there may be rain or even snow, but in many southern areas it is still warm.

1. **The best title for the story is:**
   a. Winter
   b. Birds Fly South
   c. Fall
   d. Animal Habits

2. **Before winter comes, birds may:**
   a. fly north
   b. fly south
   c. store nuts
   d. wear warm clothing

3. **Birds go to places:**
   a. with shorter days
   b. with warmer climate
   c. with more trees
   d. with more snow

4. **People prepare by:**
   a. flying south
   b. wearing warmer clothes
   c. storing food
   d. feeding birds

5. **In the story, the word "fall" means:**
   a. drop to the ground
   b. trip
   c. cold
   d. a season

6. **Animals probably know when winter is coming because:**
   a. the calendar tells them
   b. the leaves fall
   c. they seem to sense a change
   d. it snows

 FS-32044 Reading

"All that running around has made me hungry," Jimmy told Danny. "Let's make ourselves some lunch. We'll make a sandwich with everything we like best on it. Here is the bread. Now get some peanut butter and jelly. What next?"

Jimmy found a banana and put that on the bread. Then Danny got two chocolate cookies and one Mr. Twinkle cupcake and pressed them down on the banana, and to top it off, he added Captain Quack Potato Chips.

"My mouth is watering! Let's eat." Danny lifted up the sandwich. Splat! The bottom piece of bread had a hole in it. "Next time, we'll just make a ham and cheese sandwich so we won't have to clean up this mess," sighed Danny.

1. **The best name for this story would be:**

   a. Making Chocolate Chip Cookies

   b. Eating Lunch at Home

   c. A Super Sandwich

2. **Jimmy put a lot of _____ on his sandwich.**

   a. sweets

   b. straws

   c. meat

3. **What did Jimmy put on the very top?**

   a. potato chips

   b. chocolate cookies

   c. a banana

4. **"My mouth is watering!" What does this mean?**

   a. Danny is very hungry.

   b. Danny wants something to drink.

   c. Danny hurt his tooth.

5. **The story does not say, but you can tell that:**

   a. The sandwich was too heavy for the bread.

   b. Jimmy went out for lunch every day.

   c. The boys forgot to put on catsup.

FS-32044 Reading

Name _____

Dogs have been "man's best friend" for thousands of years. They have earned man's love and respect because of their faithfulness and devotion. Many dogs have given their lives to save their masters.

Dogs **guard** the home, cattle and sheep. Their keen sense of smell makes them good for hunting animals. They like to be with people and often greet us with barks and wagging tails.

Dogs were the first animals to be tamed by man and are fifth in intelligence among animals.

1. **The best title for this story is:**
   a. Hunting Dogs
   b. Pets
   c. Intelligent Animals
   d. Dogs

2. **Dogs are _____ in intelligence among animals:**
   a. first
   b. third
   c. fifth
   d. fourth

3. **They are good to take along on hunting trips because:**
   a. they like people
   b. they have a good sense of smell
   c. they like animals
   d. they enjoy trips

4. **They have earned man's love and respect because:**
   a. they are faithful and devoted
   b. we like them
   c. they were the first tame animals
   d. they have been here a long time

5. **In the story, the word "guard" means:**
   a. a man who protects things
   b. a soldier
   c. to watch over
   d. protect with a gun

6. **We can guess a dog enjoys company:**
   a. by his barks
   b. by his intelligence
   c. by his wagging tail
   d. by two of these answers

Last summer we took a **trip** to Hawaii. We boarded a jet and traveled for many hours.

In Hawaii we saw many new things. We saw a rain forest and an active volcano. We played in the sand and swam in the very warm water.

We took many photographs so we could remember our trip forever. We had to come home all too soon.

1. **The best title for this story is:**
   a. Hawaii's Climate
   b. Flying in a Jet
   c. Our Trip to Hawaii
   d. Visiting a Rain Forest

2. **The first thing the story writer did in the story was:**
   a. board the jet
   b. pack his clothes
   c. buy plane tickets
   d. plan the trip

3. **He can always remember the trip because:**
   a. they were there a long time
   b. they took many photographs
   c. it was their first trip
   d. Hawaii is a nice place to visit

4. **Because of the weather, a good item of clothing to have along would have been:**
   a. a hat
   b. item of clothing
   c. a heavy coat
   d. a ski suit

5. **In the story, the word "trip" means:**
   a. stumble
   b. fall down
   c. set off
   d. a journey

6. **From the story it sounds like the writer:**
   a. is a photographer
   b. was frightened by the volcano
   c. was sorry the trip had to end
   d. takes many trips

FS-32044 Reading

In almost every part of the world, children play with dolls. They may be made of anything from cookie dough to plastic, wood, or rubber. They may be made at home or purchased in the stores that bought the dolls from factories.

Children like to play "grownup" with their dolls. They sew for them, sing to them and even pretend the dolls can talk. Dolls are a **comfort** to the sick and amuse the well. They belong to the rich and poor alike.

1. **The best title for this story is:**
   a. Dolls of Yesterday
   b. Dolls
   c. Playthings
   d. Making Dolls

2. **The story says children use dolls to:**
   a. pretend to be grown-ups
   b. as a substitute for friends
   c. learn sewing
   d. be grown up

3. **After reading the article, we learn that dolls are most preferred by:**
   a. boys
   b. rich children
   c. poor children
   d. rich and poor alike

4. **Dolls are made from:**
   a. mostly wood
   b. many things
   c. mostly dough
   d. mostly plastic

5. **In the story, the word "comfort" means:**
   a. medicine
   b. a blanket
   c. relief from sadness
   d. happy

6. **After reading the article, we can assume:**
   a. the best dolls are made of plastic
   b. dolls may be like friends
   c. you should make your own dolls
   d. dolls were invented in America

FS-32044 Reading

Flying fish do not actually fly as birds do. The fish throws itself from the water with the motion of its strong tail. Once it is in the air it spreads large fins, which act like the wings of a glider. This glide through the air may take the fish 150 to 1,000 feet.

Flying fish live in warm seas. They generally swim in **schools**. The California flying fish grows to be about 18 inches long. Flying fish make excellent food. Many visitors to Catalina Island take a special trip to view flying fish after dark. Huge searchlights are flashed on the ocean so the fish are easy to see.

1. **A good title for this article is:**
   a. A Fish that Really Flies
   b. Flying Fish
   c. Fishing in California
   d. Warm Water Fish

2. **The flying fish doesn't actually:**
   a. swim
   b. glide
   c. fly
   d. sail

3. **The flying fish trip described above is made in:**
   a. the morning
   b. the afternoon
   c. the evening or at night
   d. any time of day

4. **Flying fish have large fins that help them:**
   a. fly
   b. swim
   c. glide through the air
   d. probably both B and C

5. **In the article, the word "schools" means:**
   a. places to learn
   b. groups
   c. large buildings
   d. areas

6. **The fish may glide as many as:**
   a. a hundred feet
   b. a hundred and fifty feet
   c. a thousand feet
   d. two hundred feet

Name _____

A circus is still a show where you can **watch** clowns doing funny tricks. You can see daring men and women on the high trapeze. Fearless people train and tame lions. Circus bands and bright costumes add to the excitement just as they did long ago.

Circuses used to travel from town to town in colorful wagons pulled by **horses**. The shows were held in tents called "big tops." Today the circus is much the **same**, but it travels by train or truck. The "big top" is gone and circus people perform in stadiums and auditoriums.

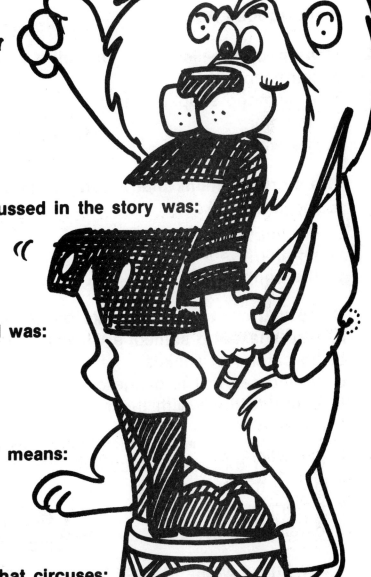

1. **The best title for this story is:**
   a. A Visit to the Circus
   b. The Circus Then and Now
   c. The New Circus
   d. Circus Acts

2. **Many circus acts:**
   a. change each week
   b. are like those of years ago
   c. are scarier now
   d. are more colorful now

3. **The first change that was discussed in the story was:**
   a. the buildings
   b. the acts
   c. the way of travel
   d. the bands

4. **The second change mentioned was:**
   a. the animals
   b. the places used for shows
   c. the trains and wagons
   d. the costumes

5. **In the story, the word "watch" means:**
   a. look at
   b. a gadget for telling time
   c. supervise
   d. take care of

6. **The article gives us the idea that circuses:**
   a. have changed a lot
   b. aren't too interesting for adults
   c. have made some changes but are still much like they were
   d. haven't changed at all

45                    FS-32044 **Reading**

One **misleading** belief about snakes is that if one has a triangular or diamond-shaped head it is poisonous. Some of the world's most dangerous snakes, such as the king cobra and the coral snake, have blunt rounded heads. On the other hand, many harmless snakes have distinct triangular shaped heads. You cannot identify a poisonous snake simply by the shape of its head. You need to get help from someone who knows snakes well.

1. **The best title for this story is:**
   a. Learning About Snakes
   b. Don't Judge a Snake by the Shape of Its Head
   c. Unusual Snakes
   d. Poisonous Animals

2. **Many people believe you can tell if a snake is poisonous by:**
   a. the shape of its head
   b. a diamond shaped mark
   c. its color
   d. the way it moves

3. **The story mentions that a dangerous snake is:**
   a. the rattlesnake
   b. the coral snake
   c. the garter snake
   d. the copperhead

4. **Since you can't judge a snake by its shape it is best to:**
   a. take snakes to someone who can identify them for you
   b. be careful of snakes
   c. test to see if it is dangerous
   d. compare them with those you remember

5. **In this story, the word "misleading" means:**
   a. going in the wrong direction
   b. giving the wrong idea
   c. leading away
   d. careless movement

6. **If you find a snake in your yard, the best way to deal with it would be:**
   a. call a parent
   b. leave it alone
   c. get another grown-up if your parents are away
   d. all of these

FS-32044 Reading

Name _____

| 1 c. margarine | 1 tsp. vanilla | **Table of Measures** |
| 1 c. sugar | 3 c. sifted flour | tsp. = teaspoon |
| 2 eggs | 1 tsp. salt | c. = cup |

**Cream** butter or margarine until soft. Add sugar and **cream** again. Beat in eggs and vanilla. Sift in flour and salt then blend together. Chill for two or three hours. Use cookie cutters to cut dough into fancy shapes. Bake at 350 degrees for ten minutes.

1. **The best title for the information above is:**
   a. Recipe for Cut Cookies
   b. How to Mix Dough
   c. How to Cut Cookies
   d. Ingredients We Need

2. **The c. stands for:**
   a. cut
   b. cube
   c. cup or cups
   d. can

3. **The first thing to do is:**
   a. add the eggs
   b. sift the flour
   c. chill the dough
   d. cream the butter

4. **Just before you cut the cookies you should:**
   a. add the flour and salt
   b. chill the dough
   c. add the sugar
   d. bake the cookies

5. **The word "cream" means:**
   a. wipe out
   b. mix until creamy
   c. add milk or water
   d. add a little cream

6. **The recipe should be followed carefully because:**
   a. there is only one way to make cookies
   b. these are the best cookies you can make
   c. using the wrong amounts could spoil the cookies
   d. someone might know if you don't follow it carefully

FS-32044 Reading

In Alaska and other parts of the far North, the sun does not set at all during the summer months. **In spite of** this, the summers remain cool. This is partly because the sun remains low in the sky. It does not rise **straight** overhead.

Can you imagine what it would be like to live in this area? How would you know when to sleep or play? Would you like to visit an area where the sun does not set?

Do you think the "Land of the Midnight Sun" is a good name for Alaska?

1. **The best title for this article is:**
   a. A Trip to Alaska
   b. Northern Summers
   c. Sun Overhead
   d. Summertime

2. **Because the sun remains low during the summer, the far north remains:**
   a. cool
   b. hot
   c. dark
   d. warm

3. **From this story, we realize why Alaska is sometimes called:**
   a. Constant Day
   b. The Coldest Land
   c. Land of the Midnight Sun
   d. A Land of Snow

4. **In the story, "in spite of" means:**
   a. because of
   b. dislike of
   c. even though this happens
   d. when this happens

5. **The word "straight," as used above, means:**
   a. directly
   b. a narrow passage of water
   c. almost
   d. not crooked

6. **A good way to know when to sleep in Alaska would be:**
   a. watch a calendar
   b. check the clock
   c. wait till you are sleepy
   d. go to bed at sunset.

FS-32044 Reading

**Name** _____

"We missed you at school last Tuesday, Chip," Mrs. Decker said. "How did you break your arm, falling out of a tree? Sit down and tell me what happened to you."

"Two nights ago, when it was very late and I was sound asleep, an alligator came through my window. He was just about to take a big bite out of my toe when I spotted him at the bottom of my bed. So I jumped up and started to bark like a dog. That alligator sure hurried to get out the window again, but I forgot to move out of his way and he knocked me over with his tail. When I opened my eyes, there I was lying on the floor. From now on, I'm going to lock my window at night!"

1. **A good name for this story would be:**

   a. Chip Breaks His Arm
   b. An Alligator Eats Chip
   c. Barking Scares Alligators

2. **Chip tried to** _____ **the alligator.**

   a. bite
   b. scare
   c. make friends with

3. **When did the alligator come through the window?**

   a. in the afternoon
   b. on Monday
   c. very late

4. **Tail means "something that wags." Tale means:**

   a. a story
   b. a test
   c. a book

5. **The story does not say, but you can guess that**

   a. Chip was having a nightmare.
   b. Chip lived in the jungle.
   c. Chip did not really have a broken arm.

Mr. Anderson bought a camera for his son Scott. Scott went down the street and started shooting pictures. Suddenly, he heard someone scream.

"Stop that thief; he has my dog," yelled a woman.

Scott saw a man dashing down the street. The man was holding a silver poodle. Scott put his foot in the man's **path** as he ran past. The man dropped the dog.

The man jumped up and ran away, but Scott got a picture of him before he disappeared. The woman thanked Scott for his help.

1.  **The most interesting title for this story is:**
    a. Scott and His Camera
    b. Scott Gets a Present
    c. The Boy Who Saved a Dog
    d. A Happy Day

2.  **Scott was on the street when a dog was stolen because:**
    a. he liked to play outside
    b. his father told him to go
    c. he heard someone scream
    d. he was trying his new camera

3.  **When Scott tripped the man and later took his picture, it proved:**
    a. he could think quickly
    b. he was good with a camera
    c. he liked dogs
    d. he always helped others

4.  **The lady thanked Scott because:**
    a. he was a friend of hers
    b. he saved her dog
    c. the picture helped catch the thief
    d. he took her picture

5.  **In this story, the word "path" means:**
    a. a walkway
    b. a direction of traveling
    c. a road made by traveling an area often
    d. a way of life

6.  **Even though what Scott did turned out well:**
    a.  it was perfectly safe
    b.  it could have been dangerous
    c.  it would be good to try
    d.  it would be good for everyone to do

     FS-32044 Reading

Grizzly bears are massive animals native to western North America. Large numbers of these great beasts once roamed the western states, but only a few hundred remain in the United States today.

Grizzly bears may grow up to 8 feet tall and weigh 800 pounds. These bears are, of course, very frightening. Their coat varies from creamy brown to almost black. Their **limbs** are dark. Their fur is often tipped with white and thus they are sometimes called silver-tips.

Although few of these bears remain in the United States, more of them live in Alaska and Canada.

1. **The most interesting title for this story would be:**
   a. Grizzly Bears
   b. The Disappearing Grizzly
   c. Bears of North America
   d. In the Woods

2. **A very frightening thing about a grizzly can be his:**
   a. cry
   b. size
   c. fur
   d. color

3. **The bears are sometimes called silver tips because:**
   a. their fur is tipped with silver
   b. they live in a land of silver
   c. they have a touch of white on their fur that may look like silver
   d. their ears have silver tips

4. **There are now:**
   a. more grizzlies in North America
   b. less grizzlies in the United States
   c. more bears in Mexico
   d. fewer bears in Alaska

5. **In the story, the word "limbs" means:**
   a. parts of a tree
   b. arms
   c. legs
   d. parts similar to arms and legs

6. **We can assume that a grizzly would be:**
   a. very dangerous
   b. very popular
   c. found mainly in South America
   d. friendly

Name _____

As we were driving along the **deserted** country road, we saw a spooky house. There seemed to be a face peering at us from a window. We began to shake with fear. Suddenly our car stopped. We had run out of gas. There seemed to be no place to go, so with our teeth chattering, we approached the scary house. The door was open. We went in.

Something bumped into me and I spun around. I realized that it was only an old cow that had been trapped inside accidentally.

1. **The best title for this story is:**
   a. A Trip to the Country
   b. A Spooky Adventure
   c. Faces in the Night
   d. Chattering Teeth

2. **The face peered from the:**
   a. door
   b. barn
   c. window
   d. basement

3. **The writer's teeth were chattering because:**
   a. he was cold
   b. he was scared
   c. he was trying to make noise
   d. he had a toothache

4. **The cow:**
   a. couldn't find a way out
   b. lived in the house
   c. liked warm places
   d. came in to scare someone

5. **In the story, the word "deserted" means:**
   a. a dry land
   b. a sweet food
   c. abandoned
   d. scary

6. **The writer probably entered the spooky house:**
   a. to phone for or get help
   b. because he likes scary places
   c. for fun
   d. because he wanted to rest

FS-32044 Reading

Scientists have **advanced** many reasons to explain why dinosaurs died out. The main cause was probably the rise of mountain ranges during the Cretaceous period. When mountains formed, great seaways drained the vast swamplands and they dried up. This caused many changes in climate and food supply. The dinosaurs could not adjust. The plant eaters could not eat the new plants so many died. Then those that ate the plant eaters did not have enough food. This long slow process took about 10 to 20 million years.

1. **The best title for this story is:**
   a. What Dinosaurs Ate
   b. Living Long Ago
   c. Why Dinosaurs Died Off
   d. How Mountains Formed

2. **Many dinosaurs didn't have food because:**
   a. other animals ate it
   b. the swamplands dried up
   c. the seas became larger
   d. all the food was soured

3. **Meat eating dinosaurs died because:**
   a. the plant eaters died
   b. they ate plants
   c. the animals were in the hills
   d. they ate too much

4. **This long process took about:**
   a. 5 million years
   b. 1 to 2 million years
   c. 25 million years
   d. 10 to 20 million years

5. **In the story, the word "advanced" means:**
   a. walked forward
   b. suggested or proposed
   c. moved ahead in space
   d. know for sure

6. **The information man has written about dinosaurs is:**
   a. all true
   b. just a story for children
   c. assumed from things people have found
   d. mostly false

 FS-32044 Reading

No movement of any animal, even the swift gait of the cheetah, is more graceful than the slithering flow of the snake. Armless and legless, he moves across the surface of the ground or climbs trees with great ease.

As we watch we can soon understand how he moves. First the tail is held against a rough spot. Next the forward part of his body is stretched until it touches another rough spot. If he can hold this spot with a part of his body, his tail can then be **drawn** up and placed at this spot too and in this way the snake can be pulled forward.

1. **The best title for this story is:**
   a. How Animals Move
   b. How a Snake Moves
   c. Snakes
   d. Graceful Animals

2. **The author feels that:**
   a. cheetahs are the most graceful
   b. most animals move with ease
   c. it is hard to learn how snakes move
   d. the movement of snakes is graceful

3. **It is surprising that snakes move as well as they do because:**
   a. they aren't very smart
   b. other animals are faster
   c. they have no arms or legs
   d. many things get in the way

4. **According to the story we can learn more about snake's movements by:**
   a. reading about them
   b. watching them
   c. raising them
   d. playing with them

5. **In the story the word "drawn" means:**
   a. pushed
   b. pulled
   c. sketched
   d. drawn with a pencil

6. **Even though the story says snakes are graceful to watch, we know:**
   a. they all make good pets
   b. everyone should watch them
   c. some are dangerous
   d. they are faster than most animals

Name _____

The metric system is a group of units used to make any kind of measurement. It is said to be one of the simplest of measurements ever used. The metric system is used in all major countries with the exception of the United States.

The metric system was created by French scientists in the 1790's. The word metric comes from the basic unit of length in the system, the meter.

The metric system may **seem** difficult if you have not used it. This is because you are not familiar with the units. Once you use the system, it becomes easier to understand.

1. **The best title for this story is:**
   a. The Metric System
   b. New Ways to Measure
   c. Understanding Measurement
   d. The French Measurement

2. **The author suggests that:**
   a. it is hard to use this system
   b. the United States should learn the system
   c. it is easier to use the system after you are familiar with it
   d. it would probably be too hard to learn

3. **The system is popular because:**
   a. it was begun by Americans
   b. it was begun by the French
   c. it can be used for any kind of measurement
   d. everyone understands it

4. **The system originally began in:**
   a. The United States
   b. France
   c. in all countries except the U.S.
   d. England

5. **The word "seem" means:**
   a. appear to be
   b. a line of sewing
   c. is really
   d. none of these

6. **Since so many countries use the metric system, it is possible:**
   a. the U.S. may some day use it
   b. the U.S. will never use it
   c. the U.S. must use it to be popular
   d. other countries will change to our system

# A Friendly Snake

One day, I was lying under a tree. Suddenly, I felt something lick my face. I opened one eye. (Gasp! Gulp!) It was a snake. A huge green snake! He just sat there looking at me. His tongue was hanging out. Did he want to play? "Hello," I said in a brave voice. "My name is Danny." The snake slurped his tongue back in his mouth. "Hi, there," he answered. "I'm Ralph."

I was just about to scream. Then I woke up.

1. **What is the main idea of this story?**
   a. a snake that talks
   b. sleeping under a tree
   c. a funny dream
2. **Another word for <u>scream</u> is:**
   a. yell
   b. search
   c. sing
3. **Danny was very surprised because:**
   a. The snake talked.
   b. The snake was green.
   c. The snake screamed.
4. **Where was Danny lying?**
   _____
   _ _ _ _ _ _ _ _ _ _ _ _ _ _ _ _ _ _ _ _
   _____
5. **What did Ralph look like?**
   _____
   _ _ _ _ _ _ _ _ _ _ _ _ _ _ _ _ _ _ _ _
   _____
6. **Find three sounds in the story.**
   _____
   _ _ _ _ _ _ _ _ _ _ _ _ _ _ _ _ _ _ _ _
   _____

Name _____    Date _____

# A Spider's Adventure

"I want to go to the park. How am I going to cross the street?" wondered the spider. "The cars are going too fast." Just then, a shoe appeared. "Perfect! I'll pop on this shoe." Thump. Squish. Thump. Squish. The shoe started running. It went faster and faster. "Help! Let me off!" screamed the spider, but the shoe ran on and on. One hour later, it finally stopped. "I'll never take a shoe anywhere again!" sputtered the spider. "Next time, I'm taking the bus."

**1. What is the main idea of this story?**
   a. how a shoe runs
   b. a very long ride
   c. crossing the street

**2. The word <u>wonder</u> means:**
   a. to tell a secret
   b. to make a guess
   c. to think about

**3. You can guess the spider:**
   a. never got to the park
   b. didn't have any shoes
   c. didn't like the park

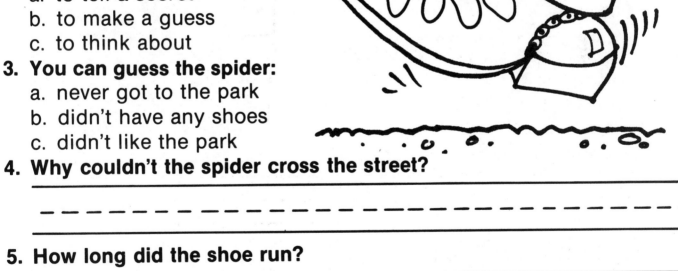

**4. Why couldn't the spider cross the street?**

_____

- - - - - - - - - - - - - - - - - - - - - - - -

_____

**5. How long did the shoe run?**

_____

- - - - - - - - - - - - - - - - - - - - - - - -

_____

**6. What sounds does a shoe make?**

_____

- - - - - - - - - - - - - - - - - - - - - - - -

_____

       FS-32044 Reading

# Little Lost Egg

One bright sunny day, a goose went out walking. She saw something under a tree. "A little lost egg!" she cried. "I'll sit on it and keep it warm." After three days, the egg cracked open. Out jumped a kangaroo. "I'll find your mother," said the goose. Away she flew. When the goose looked down, the kangaroo was gone. The goose turned around. There was the kangaroo, right behind her. He was flying! "He thinks I'm his mother. I might as well keep him. I can teach him to say 'Honk! honk!' like me."

1. **What is the main idea of this story?**
   a. a new mother
   b. a walking goose
   c. a flying kangaroo

2. **The opposite of <u>lost</u> is:**
   a. found
   b. lose
   c. forgot

3. **The kangaroo will learn how to:**
   a. look like a goose
   b. walk like a goose
   c. sound like a goose

4. **Where was the egg?**

   _____

   _____

5. **What kind of day is it in the story?**

   _____

   _____

6. **How long did the goose sit on the egg?**

   _____

   _____

# Ping-Pong, Anyone?

Ho-hum. Another day on this dusty old shelf. Doesn't anyone need a size 13 AAAA green shoe? Wait a minute. I hear a voice. "Do you have a good shoe for playing football?" a tall man asked. Uh-oh. I don't like football. I'll get stomped on! Tramped on! "Nice shoe," said the man. "But it doesn't go with my clothes." Phew! Saved! I'd make a good ping-pong shoe. I won't get hurt playing ping-pong.

1. **What is the main idea of this story?**
   a. a lonely green shoe
   b. a short green shoe
   c. shoes for games
2. **To go with means:**
   a. to hurry
   b. to match
   c. to hurt
3. **You can guess the man liked:**
   a. ping-pong
   b. playing football
   c. green shoes
4. **Where was the size 13 AAAA shoe?**

   _____

   _____

5. **Who wanted a football shoe?**

   _____

   _____

6. **Name a game that uses a ball.**

   _____

   _____

# Summer Fun!

Dear Mom and Dad,

Here I am at camp. It was a long trip yesterday. First, the bus driver got lost. He went to the wrong camp. It was for boys. Finally, we got to our camp. It was late at night. I found 300 frogs sitting in my tent. They wouldn't leave. So I left. This morning, guess what happened? My sleeping bag wouldn't unzip. I could be stuck in here forever! Camp is fun. Wish you were here.

Love,
Nancy

1. **What is the main idea of this story?**
   a. a letter to Nancy
   b. riding on a bus
   c. a letter from camp

2. **To wish means to:**
   a. have
   b. want
   c. give

3. **Nancy has been at camp:**
   a. for two days
   b. for one night
   c. a long time

4. **What was in Nancy's tent?**

_____

_____

5. **Who got lost?**

_____

_____

6. **When did Nancy get to camp?**

_____

_____

# Great Day for Moving

"Everybody up!" called Thurmond, the chief turtle. "This is moving day. Ozzie, you take the pillows. Della can pack the suitcases. The chairs and lamps will be Wally's. I'll take the piano. We'd better get going. Our new home is three blocks away. It will take us one month to get there. I hope it doesn't snow. Then it will take us two months."

1. **What is the main idea of this story?**
   a. packing up chairs
   b. getting ready to move
   c. moving in a month

2. **To pack means the same as:**
   a. fill up
   b. set out
   c. move around

3. **You can guess the turtles:**
   a. like the snow
   b. move once a year
   c. move very slowly

4. **What did Wally carry?**

   _____
   _ _ _ _ _ _ _ _ _ _ _ _ _ _ _ _ _ _ _ _ _ _
   _____

5. **How far are the turtles moving?**

   _____
   _ _ _ _ _ _ _ _ _ _ _ _ _ _ _ _ _ _ _ _ _ _
   _____

6. **Thurmond hopes it won't snow. Why?**

   _____
   _ _ _ _ _ _ _ _ _ _ _ _ _ _ _ _ _ _ _ _ _ _
   _____

# Brusha Brusha

Terri Jean works at a zoo. She has a special job. Every Monday, Terri walks into the hippo pond. "OK, Higby. Open your mouth," says Terri. "Wider! Wider! Now I can brush your teeth for you." Terri pulls out a giant toothbrush. She squeezes Plum Patootie toothpaste on it. That is Higby's favorite. It is very sweet. For ten minutes Terri rubs and scrubs. "All clean, Higby. Let me see you smile. How beautiful! Your teeth really sparkle."

HIPPOPOTAMUS

1. **What is the main idea of this story?**
   a. cleaning the hippo pond
   b. cleaning Higby's teeth
   c. a job at the zoo
2. **The word** <u>sparkle</u> **can also mean:**
   a. to brush
   b. to clean
   c. to shine
3. **Higby would probably like the taste of:**
   a. lemon
   b. pepper
   c. honey
4. **Where does Terri work?**

   _____

   _____

5. **What is Terri's job?**

   _____

   _____

6. **Name a day of the week found in the story.**

   _____

   _____

# What's for Breakfast?

Every morning, my mother makes breakfast for me. She fixes breakfast for the cat, the dog and the bird, too. Yesterday, Mother was in a big rush. She cooked everything very fast. "Barbie, breakfast is ready!" she called. There was a dog dish at my place on the table. The bird had a dish of milk. The cat had birdseed. The dog had eggs. They ate up everything! I don't like dog food. I guess I'll have some cake. (I'm glad the dog ate my eggs.)

1. **What is the main idea of this story?**
   a. what Mother cooks
   b. mixed up breakfasts
   c. mixed up animals
2. **Another word for <u>rush</u> is:**
   a. heavy
   b. hurry
   c. helper
3. **You can tell that the animals:**
   a. fix their own breakfasts
   b. like different foods
   c. always eat dinner
4. **What did the bird have?**

   _____
   - - - - - - - - - - - - - - - - -
   _____

5. **Why did the breakfasts get mixed up?**

   _____
   - - - - - - - - - - - - - - - - -
   _____

6. **Name three animals in the story.**

   _____
   - - - - - - - - - - - - - - - - -
   _____

FS-32044 Reading

**DILLY PARK PET FAIR CONTEST**

## A Bright Idea

I have a little sister named Kim. She doesn't do much. She crawls around. Sometimes she hums and even meows. Hm-m-m. That gives me an idea. I could enter Kim in a contest. The Dilly Park Pet Fair is on Sunday. I'll dress her in her furry white snowsuit. I'll pin a tail on her, too. No one will ever know she isn't a cat. What a terrific plan! I hope Kim wins the contest.

1. **What is the main idea of this story?**
   a. dressing up a cat
   b. an idea for a contest
   c. going to a pet fair
2. **Another word for idea is:**
   a. inside
   b. tight
   c. thought
3. **You can tell that Kim:**
   a. is really a cat
   b. can't walk yet
   c. can't crawl around
4. **What does Kim do during the day?**

   _____

   _ _ _ _ _ _ _ _ _ _ _ _ _ _ _ _ _ _ _ _ _

   _____

5. **Where is the pet fair?**

   _____

   _ _ _ _ _ _ _ _ _ _ _ _ _ _ _ _ _ _ _ _ _

   _____

6. **Name a day of the week that is found in the story.**

   _____

   _ _ _ _ _ _ _ _ _ _ _ _ _ _ _ _ _ _ _ _ _

   _____

# Feeling Better?

My mom went out tonight just before dark. I am babysitting my sister Judy. Judy is sick. "Will pizza make you feel better?" I asked. After two bites, Judy felt terrible. Next I fixed some gumdrop cookies. These made her really sick! Let's see . . . I have one more idea— a peanut butter and banana sandwich. That will make her all better. What a good brother I am!

**1. What is the main idea of this story?**
   a. a sick mother
   b. a thoughtful brother
   c. a pizza for dinner

**2. Another word for idea is:**
   a. plan
   b. work
   c. sick

**3. From the story you can tell:**
   a. Mother went out late.
   b. Cookies will make you well.
   c. Food made Judy sicker.

**4. What kind of sandwich did the boy make?**

_____

_____

**5. When did Mother leave?**

_____

_____

**6. What made Judy really sick?**

_____

_____

Name _____ Date _____

# Tall Tales

What is a tall tale? Many tall tales are wild stories that people just make up. They may be about a huge fish they almost caught. Tall tales are often about people who really lived long ago. Over the years, the adventures that they had just seemed to get bigger and bigger. After awhile, no one knew what was true and what wasn't. Sometimes tall tales are about people who never lived. No one knows how some of these stories got started. Tall tales are fun. Many of the stories you think just can't be true. They make us laugh. They make us wonder. Did Johnny Appleseed really plant so many trees? Did Paul Bunyan really have a blue ox? Was John Henry that strong? Every country has tall tales. The ones you will learn about in this book took place in North America.

1. **The main idea of this story is:**
   a. about Johnny and his seeds
   b. about tall tales
   c. about many countries

2. **Many tall tales are:**
   a. hard to believe
   b. about you and me
   c. sad

3. **John Henry was supposed to be**

   _____ .

4. **You can guess that:**
   a. There are not many tall tales.
   b. Tall tales are often very old.
   c. Tall tales are always about animals.

5. **Paul Bunyan had a:**
   a. blue goat
   b. yellow bird
   c. blue ox

6. **An <u>ox</u> is:**
   a. a kind of bull
   b. an apple
   c. a small person

**Brainwork!** Think about the question. Answer it on the back. Write a tall tale about a fish that got away.

FS-32044 Reading

## Johnny Appleseed

John Chapman knew everything about trees. Fruit trees were his favorite kinds of trees. Each day he saw people heading west as they passed his Pennsylvania farm. John felt sorry for these pioneers. He knew they'd see hard times. He started giving away apple seeds. This way, people could plant beautiful orchards wherever they'd go. Soon, John gave up his farm and roamed all over the country. He planted seeds and gave people the baby trees. No one called him John Chapman anymore. His name had become Johnny Appleseed forever. Johnny was a strange sight. He slept out in the open in all weather. He wore no shoes. He carried his cooking pot by wearing it on his head. Johnny had a pet wolf, too. One day Johnny died while he was tending his trees. Some folks say they still see his ghost walking through the apple orchards of Indiana and Ohio.

1. **The main idea of this story is:**
   a. a man and his wolf
   b. heading west
   c. giving away seeds and trees

2. **John Chapman became:**
   a. John Smith
   b. Johnny Appleseed
   c. Johnny Tree

3. **Johnny had a pet**

   _____ .

4. **You can tell that:**
   a. Johnny wasn't selfish.
   b. Johnny wasn't nice.
   c. Apples grow under the ground.

5. **Johnny lived in:**
   a. Pencil City
   b. Transylvania
   c. Pennsylvania

6. **Pioneers are:**
   a. settlers in new territory
   b. fruit trees
   c. teams of horses

**Brainwork!** Think about the question. Answer it on the back. What is your favorite tree? Why?

FS-32044 Reading

# John Henry

The night John Henry was born, the whole earth shook. Rivers ran upstream. He was a very big baby and weighed 44 pounds. When John Henry grew up he wanted to work on the railroad. He got a job with the C. and O. Railroad. The year was about 1870. Steam drills had just been invented. These drills would do the work the men had done before. John Henry's friends said he could do a faster, better job than any steam drill. A contest was held. John Henry took his hammer and drilled two holes seven feet deep. The steam drill only drilled one hole nine feet deep. John Henry won. He was a great hero, but had worked too hard to win. The next day he died. John Henry's ghost was seen wandering in the mountains. Many folks claimed they even heard his hammer ringing away.

**1. The main idea of this story is:**
   a. a big hammer
   b. a railroad hero
   c. a steam drill

**2. When John Henry was a baby:**
   a. He wasn't tiny.
   b. He cried a lot.
   c. He worked on the railroad.

**3. Who won the contest?**

   _____ .

**4. You can tell that:**
   a. John Henry was lazy.
   b. John Henry was weak.
   c. John Henry's friends liked him.

**5. John Henry drilled:**
   a. a well
   b. two holes, each seven feet deep
   c. for oil

**6. A <u>hero</u> is:**
   a. someone who does great things
   b. a person who is tall
   c. a big hammer

**Brainwork!** Think about the question and answer it on the back. Why did John Henry want to show that he could work faster than a machine?

# Rip Van Winkle

If you think you like to sleep a lot, just listen to this story. "Rip Van Winkle" is an old tale from the Catskill mountains of New York. One day, Rip walked to the woods to get away from his wife. She scolded him all the time. Rip saw strange little men in the woods. They offered him a drink. He fell asleep. When he woke up, he felt stiff. Rip walked back to his village, but the place had changed. He saw no one he knew. Finally, Rip found out the truth. He had taken a nap for twenty years! Rip found his daughter. She was so happy to see her father. Rip's wife had been dead for years. He went to live with his daughter. He told his strange story over and over again for many happy years.

1. **The main idea of this story is:**
   a. a lost daughter
   b. a long sleep
   c. strange little men

2. **Rip found some men:**
   a. in the forest
   b. on his farm
   c. in his house

3. **Rip went to live with**

   _____ .

4. **When Rip woke up he probably was:**
   a. young
   b. old
   c. fat

5. **Rip's wife used to:**
   a. cook good meals
   b. bake cookies
   c. scold her husband

**Brainwork!** Think about the question. Answer it on the back. What would be bad about sleeping for twenty years?

# Paul Bunyan

This is just one story about the biggest, strongest man anywhere. Paul Bunyan was a lumberjack. He could cut down more trees than anyone. Paul and his giant blue ox, Babe, chopped down trees. They cut them into logs and took them to the sawmills. Paul even changed the map of America. Once, on a walk to Louisiana, Paul got sand in his shoes. He dumped out the sand. That pile of sand grew to be the Kiamichi Mountains of Oklahoma. Babe helped, too. When he walked he made very large footprints. People think that dinosaurs made them, but it was Babe, of course. One day, Babe got very sick. Paul cried. His tears made the Great Salt Lake of Utah! One day Babe knocked over a big tank of water. Paul dug a big ditch for the water. That ditch is known as the Mississippi River! The dirt that came from the ditch made the Rocky Mountains!

**1. The main idea of this story is:**
   a. a big ox
   b. a great man
   c. a big ditch

**2. Paul cried when:**
   a. Babe didn't feel well.
   b. He saw dinosaurs.
   c. He got sand in his shoes.

**3. Paul Bunyan was a**

   _____ .

**4. You can tell that:**
   a. Paul was lazy.
   b. Paul kept himself busy.
   c. Babe was a red ox.

**5. Babe's footprints looked like:**
   a. Paul's footprints
   b. logs
   c. dinosaur footprints

**6. A lumberjack:**
   a. bakes cakes
   b. traps bears
   c. cuts down trees

**Brainwork!** Think about the question. Answer it on the back. Write why you think Paul Bunyan could or couldn't have done all those great deeds.

70

# Davy Crockett

Davy was a real person. Tall tales about him were started by Davy himself! Davy once said that he'd killed 105 bears in eight months! By the time Davy died at the Alamo in 1836, he was thought of as a superman!

One day, Davy Crockett said, "Did you ever hear about when I fixed the sun?" His friends shook their heads. They knew this was going to be a good story. "Well," Davy went on, "one day the weather was so cold that everything was frozen solid. The sun was stuck between two pieces of ice. If I didn't get it unstuck fast, everyone would be done for. Well, I took a bear that I'd just killed. I started hitting the ice with it. In about fifteen seconds, the sun got loose. The sun walked up to me and saluted. I put a piece of the sun into my pocket. I carried it along to show everyone the fresh daylight."

1. **The main idea of this story is:**
   a. a frozen bear
   b. Davy and the sun
   c. a man who was stuck

2. **The sun couldn't get out of:**
   a. bed
   b. the clouds
   c. some ice

3. **Davy said he'd killed**

   _____ .

4. **You can guess that:**
   a. Davy didn't talk much.
   b. Davy liked to brag.
   c. Davy was a bear.

5. **Most of the stories were:**
   a. started by Davy
   b. told by bears
   c. told by Davy's mother

6. **Saluted means:**
   a. greeted
   b. smiled
   c. stepped on

**Brainwork!** Think about the question. Answer it on the back. Why do you think that Davy's story isn't true?

71

Name _____ Date _____

## St. Patrick of Erie

The Erie Canal linked the Hudson River to Lake Erie. Building the canal was very hard work. The canal was built mainly by Irish people who came to America.

There was one big problem after the canal was built. Snakes were all over the waterway. Once a man fell in. He was pretty dirty. So dirty, in fact, that all the snakes around him died. They were poisoned! That gave an Irishman named Joe an idea. There are no snakes in Ireland. St. Patrick got rid of them hundreds of years ago. Well, this Irishman named Joe decided that snakes are afraid of Irish dirt. In those days, most Irishmen carried some dirt from Ireland with them. They started throwing some of it overboard. It landed on the banks of the canal. The snakes died. Since then, there aren't many snakes on or near the Erie Canal! Joe was called the "St. Patrick of Erie".

1. **The main idea of this story is:**
   a. getting rid of snakes
   b. dirty snakes
   c. building a canal

2. **The Erie Canal hasn't many:**
   a. boats
   b. snakes
   c. fish

3. **Joe was called**

   _____ .

4. **You can tell that:**
   a. Joe liked snakes.
   b. Many people didn't like snakes.
   c. Snakes like dirt.

5. **The Erie Canal was built by:**
   a. Frenchmen
   b. Chinese workers
   c. Irishmen

6. **A <u>canal</u> is:**
   a. a river
   b. a manmade waterway
   c. a big boat

**Brainwork!** Think about the question. Answer it on the back. Write about why you do or don't like snakes.

72

Name _____ Date _____

# Mike Fink

"I love to fight! I'm part wild horse and alligator." Mike Fink, of course, was really a man. He was also the most famous river boatman. Mike bragged a lot about himself. He said, "I can outrun, outshoot, outbrag and outfight any man on the Mississippi River." Mike was always fighting with other boatmen. He even tangled with the great Davy Crockett a few times. One story tells about a shooting contest they had. Each man claimed his gun was best. Davy won that contest. Another time Mike said he could beat Davy in a boat race. Davy beat Mike in that one, too. They ended up as friends. Mike's daughter was just like her father. He sure was proud of her! Writers in the 1800's loved to tell tales about Mike Fink, the most daring of all the boatmen!

1. **The main idea of this story is:**
   a. about Davy Crockett
   b. Mike Fink's daughter
   c. a famous boatman

2. **Mike Fink said he could:**
   a. beat anyone at anything
   b. go around the world
   c. whinny like a horse

3. **Mike Fink was proud of**

    .

4. **You can guess that:**
   a. No one liked Mike.
   b. People liked Mike's adventures.
   c. Mike didn't have children.

5. **Mike had contests with:**
   a. Daniel Boone
   b. Paul Bunyan
   c. Davy Crockett

6. **To <u>capture</u> means:**
   a. fight with
   b. catch
   c. set free

**Brainwork!** Think about the question. Answer it on the back. Why do people like to brag about themselves?

FS-32044 Reading

Name _____    Date _____

# Joe Magarac

Joe was the greatest steel man that ever lived. He worked in Pennsylvania. There, most of America's steel is made. Joe was the biggest, toughest steel man. He would stir the boiling hot steel by hand. Then he'd take it and shape it into bars. No one else could do that. Joe ate five meals a day. The rest of the time he'd make steel. Joe made so much steel that his friends got angry. They thought they'd lose their jobs. Joe made all the steel needed. Joe just smiled. "No," he said. "All of America needs steel. We'll just build a bigger mill." But the steel mill was closed. Joe was sad. One day, he jumped into the steel pot. After he melted down, people could hear him laugh. Joe had made the world's strongest steel. A new mill was built. There were enough jobs for everyone. Today, good steel men call each other "magaracs".

1. **The main idea of this story is:**
   a. a big mill
   b. a man who loved steel
   c. a big eater

2. **Joe Magarac:**
   a. did the work of many men
   b. was lazy
   c. didn't eat much

3. **Joe made the world's strongest**

   _____ .

4. **You can guess that:**
   a. Joe was a real person.
   b. Joe didn't like hamburgers.
   c. No one would jump into a steel pot.

5. **Steel men sometimes call each other:**
   a. mills
   b. steel pots
   c. magaracs

6. **A <u>mill</u> is:**
   a. a place to eat lunch
   b. a building in which steel is made
   c. a kind of steel

**Brainwork!** Think about the question. Answer it on the back. Why did steel workers make up the story about Joe Magarac?

74

# Jean Lafitte the Pirate

Ships that sailed off the coast of Louisiana weren't safe. Their biggest danger was pirate Jean Lafitte. Jean didn't care whose ships he attacked. He did, however, love the United States. Jean told President Jackson he'd help him fight the British. This was during the War of 1812. At first, the president didn't want the help of a pirate! Later, he changed his mind. Jean Lafitte and his men fought bravely. Lafitte became a hero. He had saved New Orleans from the British! After the war, Jean went back to being a pirate. After he died, many people tried to find his treasure of gold and jewels. Once, a soldier said he saw the ghost of Lafitte. The ghost told him where his treasure was. He told him to use it to help people. The soldier ran to town and told everyone. When they raced back to the spot, there was no treasure. They just heard a ghost moaning. The soldier shouldn't have told Jean's secret.

1. **The main idea of this story is:**
   a. buried treasure
   b. the life of a pirate
   c. running from a ghost

2. **Jean Lafitte wanted to:**
   a. help the British
   b. look for a gold mine
   c. help the Americans

3. **The soldier told**

   _____ .

4. **You can tell that:**
   a. Jean Lafitte was a president.
   b. Jean liked the life of a pirate.
   c. The British liked Jean.

5. **Jean Lafitte attacked:**
   a. airplanes
   b. trains
   c. ships

6. **Moaning is:**
   a. laughing and giggling
   b. yawning out loud
   c. a long, sad sound

**Brainwork!** Think about the question. Answer it on the back. What would you do with Jean Lafitte's treasure if you found it?

FS-32044 Reading

# Febold Feboldson

Poor Febold really was a nice man. He always tried to help people. His helping never turned out right, though. Once, Febold wanted to get rid of coyotes in Nebraska. He bought some huggags. Now, these animals will take care of all your coyote troubles. They do like to lean on trees, though. There were no trees in Nebraska. Those huggags kept falling down. They were useless against coyotes.

Another time, Febold wanted settlers in Nebraska. He heard people liked gold. He put thousands of goldfish in a river. People riding by thought that gold shine was real gold. They stayed and settled in Nebraska. When they found out what Febold had done, they were mad! Febold did start rain, though. He tricked some frogs into croaking. Everyone knows that brings rain. The people of Nebraska liked Febold for doing that!

**1. The main idea of this story is:**
   a. a bunch of frogs
   b. a strange man
   c. about trees

**2. Febold didn't have:**
   a. any animals
   b. good luck
   c. goldfish

**3. Febold lived in**

   _____ .

**4. You can tell that:**
   a. Febold didn't like people.
   b. People like coyotes.
   c. Febold meant well.

**5. Febold's strange animal was a:**
   a. teddy bear
   b. huggy bear
   c. huggag

**6. A coyote is:**
   a. a river
   b. a wild, dog-like animal
   c. an elephant

**Brainwork!** Think about the question. Answer it on the back. Draw a picture of what you think a huggag looks like.

       FS-32044 Reading

# Pecos Bill

Pecos Bill was a western hero. He was, in fact, the most famous man in the country. Bill invented roping. Bill used to rope everything around. He'd lasso the buzzards and eagles in the sky. He pulled them right down to the ground. Pecos Bill roped bears, wolves, elk and buffalo. He thought a train was a strange kind of animal. He roped it and almost wrecked it, too. Bill's horse was as tough as Bill. He ate barbed wire. That made him tough and mean. Once, Pecos Bill made a bet. He said he could ride a cyclone. He lassoed it over Kansas. That cyclone couldn't throw Bill off. Finally, it gave up and just turned into rain. Pecos Bill had the biggest ranch in the west. He needed water for his cattle. Bill dug the Rio Grande. He filled it with water from the Gulf of Mexico.

**1. The main idea of this story is:**
   a. about horses
   b. about rain
   c. about a western hero

**2. Pecos Bill liked to use:**
   a. his spurs
   b. his rope
   c. big saddles

**3. Pecos Bill dug**

   _____ .

**4. You can tell that:**
   a. Bill was an unusual man.
   b. Bill was afraid of horses.
   c. Bill knew all about trains.

**5. Bill lassoed the cyclone over:**
   a. Texas
   b. Kansas
   c. Arizona

**6. A <u>cyclone</u> is:**
   a. a big cloud
   b. a snowstorm
   c. a big wind

**Brainwork!** Think about the question. Answer it on the back. What would be useful about being a champion roper?

Name _____ Date _____

# Kemp Morgan

Kemp Morgan was quite a man! He was the most famous man in Oklahoma. He was, in fact, the man who discovered oil! In Kemp's oilfields, there was no crew. Kemp was the only worker. He could do everything himself. Kemp found oil this way: he'd walk around the fields. He'd keep his nose near the ground. Sometimes Kemp would stop. He'd sniff and sniff. He'd know by the smell if there was oil below. Kemp would dig for oil. He was always right. Often, Kemp would buy the land with the oil smell. Sometimes he'd give it away to others. Kemp just liked to smell oil for fun. When Kemp would dig a well he'd start with a shovel. Then he'd shoot the hole even bigger with his gun. He'd drill for the oil himself. Finally, he'd build tanks for the oil and put a cap on the well.

**1. The main idea of this story is:**
   a. an oily smell
   b. a man who loved oil
   c. drilling for water

**2. Sometimes Kemp would:**
   a. ask others to help him
   b. keep the land for himself
   c. get a cold

**3. Kemp kept his nose**

   _____ .

**4. You can guess that:**
   a. Kemp knew a lot about oil.
   b. Kemp had a bad sense of smell.
   c. Oil has no smell.

**5. Kemp was famous in:**
   a. New York
   b. Alaska
   c. Oklahoma

**6. A <u>crew</u> is:**
   a. an oil well
   b. a big tank
   c. a group of people working together

**Brainwork!** Think about the question. Answer it on the back. What are your favorite things to smell? Make a list of them.

78

# A.B. Stormalong

He sure was tall! Stormalong stood thirty feet tall, in fact. He signed on as a sailor on the Lady of the Sea. The captain was glad to have such a giant on board. Old Stormalong's size and strength helped him on the sea. He didn't have to climb to set the sails. He'd just reach up high and do it. Stormalong ate too much, though. For lunch he liked a rowboat full of soup. Once, the crew couldn't get the ship started. Old Stormy jumped overboard to have a look. Then he disappeared. Soon, the crew saw a huge, black octopus arm in the air. They were all mighty scared. No man could fight a thing like that! But, suddenly, Old Stormalong climbed back on board! He wasn't even hurt! "Wow!" he sighed. "That old octopus had one hundred arms! Fifty of them were trying to hold the boat down. The others were trying to hold me down! I fixed him, though. I tied every one of those arms in a double knot." Everyone cheered.

1. **The main idea of this story is:**
   a. some small fish
   b. jumping overboard
   c. a great sailor

2. **After the fight, Stormalong:**
   a. got back on the ship
   b. sank to the bottom
   c. made friends with the octopus

3. **Stormy tied the octopus' arms**

   _____ .

4. **You can tell that Stormy was:**
   a. afraid of fish
   b. very brave
   c. short

5. **How many arms did the octopus have?**
   a. none
   b. one hundred
   c. fifty

6. **An** <u>octopus</u> **is really:**
   a. a sea creature with eight arms
   b. a fish with many fins
   c. a kind of shark

**Brainwork!** Think about the question. Answer it on the back. Why did Stormalong say that the octopus had so many arms?

FS-32044 Reading

Name _____ Date _____

# Finn MacCool

Old Man Mazuma had a problem. He wanted water to go into the desert. That way, plants could bloom. Mazuma lived near the river between the United States and Mexico. It is called the Rio Grande. "Let me think," said Mazuma. "I need the world's greatest engineer." Mazuma talked to lots of folks. They all said that the man he needed was Finn MacCool. Finn was the biggest man Mazuma had ever seen. He could leap over a hill in just one leap! Finn had even built the Great Wall of China, people said. Finn carefully made his plans. He hired Irish and Chinese workers. Finn and his men dug a huge ditch. The Colorado River started to run through it. Finn was so pleased with his work. He smiled and said, "What a Grand Canyon!" And that's what it's called to this day!

1. **The main idea of this story is:**
   a. the Great Wall of China
   b. the greatest engineer
   c. a river in Mexico

2. **Old Man Mazuma needed:**
   a. water in the desert
   b. a shovel
   c. a Chinese worker

3. **Finn called his ditch**

   _____ .

4. **You can tell that:**
   a. Finn didn't like Mazuma.
   b. Finn liked his work.
   c. Finn was tiny.

5. **How did Finn get over a hill?**
   a. He drove a car.
   b. He flew over it.
   c. He leaped over in one leap.

6. **An <u>engineer</u> is:**
   a. someone who plants seeds
   b. someone who runs over hills
   c. someone who plans and builds things

**Brainwork!** Think about the question. Answer it on the back. Do you think Finn really made the Grand Canyon? Why or why not?

80

# Captain Kidd

Long ago, there were pirates along the eastern coast of America. Captain Kidd was a sailor from New York. He said he'd sail off and catch some pirates. When Captain Kidd found the pirates, he was surprised. They seemed to be having so much fun! Captain Kidd said to himself, "I think I'll become a pirate, too. But I'll keep it a secret." When Captain Kidd wanted to go back to New York, though, he couldn't. Everybody knew that he'd become a pirate. The king's soldiers were after him. The captain kept robbing ships. He had stolen lots of gold and jewels. Finally, the soldiers caught up with him. Captain Kidd was killed. People knew he had hidden his treasures. They were buried in New York and New Jersey. Every time someone got close to them, they were frightened away. Captain Kidd had sent terrible, ugly ghosts to guard the treasures. People don't give up easily, though. The treasures of Captain Kidd are still buried somewhere. If you find one, be careful of those ghosts!

**1. The main idea of this story is:**
   a. the king's soldiers
   b. a pirate and his treasure
   c. sailing a ship

**2. Captain Kidd thought that:**
   a. The life of a pirate looked great.
   b. Pirates wore dirty clothes.
   c. He didn't like gold.

**3. Captain Kidd's treasure is guarded by**

_____ .

**4. You can tell that Captain Kidd:**
   a. still sails the sea
   b. didn't want you to have his treasure
   c. gave his treasure away

**5. Captain Kidd's treasure is in:**
   a. California
   b. North and South Dakota
   c. New York and New Jersey

**6. Treasure is:**
   a. junk
   b. something that's worth a lot
   c. only gold

**Brainwork!** Think about the question. Answer it on the back. Why do you think Captain Kidd doesn't want anyone to have his treasure?

81

# Paul Bunyan and Babe Go West

Paul Bunyan had cleared all the land of North Dakota. He planted a seed of corn. It grew way up to the sky. Paul's friend Ole climbed it. His head disappeared into the clouds. Suddenly Ole shouted, "Paul! From up here I see a big ocean! I see a great land of big trees." Ole had seen the Pacific. Paul decided that he and Babe should go west. On the long trip, Babe got thirsty. Paul dug a well. Was he surprised! Boiling hot water gushed out of the well. Paul saw that it did that every hour. "I'll call it Old Faithful," he said. You can still see Old Faithful in Yellowstone Park today. Paul kept going and finally reached Washington. The trees were ready for cutting. Then he'd send the logs to China. So Paul had to dig out a river that went straight to the Pacific Ocean. He called it the Columbia River. Those logs sailed right over to China! Paul Bunyan sure was the biggest, strongest man that ever lived!

1. **The main idea of this story is:**
   a. trees from China
   b. digging a well
   c. a great logger

2. **Paul wanted to go west to:**
   a. sail to China
   b. cut trees
   c. plant corn

3. **Paul's friend Ole saw**

   _____ .

4. **You can tell that:**
   a. Paul didn't like to travel.
   b. Paul liked Babe.
   c. Paul was a farmer.

5. **Paul called the well:**
   a. Old Well
   b. Old Yellowstone
   c. Old Faithful

6. **A logger:**
   a. cuts trees down
   b. sits on logs all the time
   c. helps beavers cut logs

**Brainwork!** Think about the question. Answer it on the back. What could you see from the top of a giant corn plant?

# Tony Beaver

Tony was the most famous logger in the South. He did everything in a big way. Once, Tony decided to grow peanuts. (He called them goobers.) Well, Tony just grew too many goobers. That year, his maple trees had too much sap, too. So, Tony was stuck with molasses from the maple sap. It started to rain. Tony's town was flooded. Tony's neighbors asked him to stop the flood. Tony and his friends took the goobers out of their shells. They dumped them into the overflowing Eel River. Next, they dumped in the molasses. The sun came out. It was so hot that the river started boiling. The smell coming from the river made everyone hungry. Tony began mixing the goobers, molasses and river. He stirred for hours. Tony cooled the river. The mixture hardened. Tony took it out. He broke it into pieces. Everyone in town wanted to taste it. It was great. Tony had saved the town. He had also invented peanut brittle!

**1. The main idea of this story is:**
   a. a hero and inventor
   b. about sap
   c. a boiling river

**2. Tony's neighbors knew:**
   a. He didn't like goobers.
   b. He could help them.
   c. He couldn't swim.

**3. What did Tony invent?**

   _____ .

**4. You can tell that:**
   a. Tony's town was big.
   b. Tony couldn't help anyone.
   c. Tony was very smart.

**5. The river started boiling when:**
   a. The sun came out.
   b. Tony cut down some trees.
   c. The weather got cold.

**6. Sap is:**
   a. boiling river water
   b. a sticky liquid in trees
   c. a flood

**Brainwork!** Think about the question. Answer it on the back. Tell what you think peanut brittle tastes like.

# John Darling

When John was a little boy, there was nothing special about him. But when he got older, he chopped down a tree. He even split the stump of the tree. Was John surprised! The stump grew together again after he'd split it! John thought it was magic. He knew it meant he'd be a great man. John went to work on the Erie Canal. He had a fine boat. John wanted to marry a girl named Sal. Sal said she'd marry the man who caught the most fish. John's friends were catching lots of fish. John didn't even have one. Suddenly, he had an idea. Sal was with him on the boat. She had the reddest, shiniest hair. John told her to lean her head over the side. She did. The fish liked the light from Sal's hair. They jumped right into the boat! Soon, John Darling had a boat full of fish. A while later, he also had a wife named Sal.

1. **The main idea of this story is:**
   a. catching fish
   b. a boatman on the Erie Canal
   c. building a canal

2. **John knew that:**
   a. Someday he'd be important.
   b. Sal didn't like fish.
   c. He'd never marry Sal.

3. **Why did the fish jump into the boat?**

   _____ .

4. **You can guess that:**
   a. John couldn't chop trees down.
   b. Sal got seasick.
   c. Sal thought John was a smart man.

5. **What kind of hair did Sal have?**
   a. blond and curly
   b. red and shiny
   c. black and short

6. **A <u>stump</u> of a tree is:**
   a. the part that's left after cutting
   b. a bunch of leaves
   c. a branch

**Brainwork!** Think about the question. Answer it on the back. Why do you think this story is true or not true?

84                    FS-32044 **Reading**

# Iguanodon

It was a warm spring day in 1822. While walking down a hill, Mary Mantell noticed a strange looking rock. "These look like teeth," Mary said. Mary showed the rock to her husband. He was a paleontologist, a person who studies fossils and ancient life forms.

"These are fossils," stated Dr. Mantell. "They look like the teeth of a giant iguana lizard. This is an amazing discovery! Let's see if we can find more fossils." In time, the Mantells found many giant-sized bones. They put the bones together like a puzzle. The giant creature was called Iguanodon.

During the 1800s, thousands more fossils were found throughout the world. These creatures came to be called dinosaurs, which means "terrible lizards."

1. A good title for this story is:
   a. Digging Up Rocks
   b. The Discovery of Giant Bones
   c. How Fossil Teeth Look

2. What did Mary Mantell discover?

_____

3. Dinosaurs were called "terrible lizards" because:
   a. They crawled on the ground.
   b. They had long tails.
   c. They looked like giant monsters.

4. How did Dr. Mantell feel about Mary's discovery?

_____

**Brainwork:** Would you like to spend one year digging for dinosaur bones in the desert? Tell why or why not.

# Dinosaur Words

These words will teach you more about dinosaurs. Look up the words in your dictionary. Write each definition on the lines. Keep this page in your desk. It will help you remember the words when you are doing other pages in this book.

1. fossil: _____

_____

_____

2. reptile: _____

_____

_____

3. prehistoric: _____

_____

_____

4. extinct: _____

_____

_____

5. dinosaur: _____

_____

_____

**Look up the underlined words in your dictionary. Then complete the sentences.**

6. Tyrannosaurus Rex was the largest underlined carnivore.

It ate: _____

7. Animals with vertebrae have: _____

Name _____

# Baby Dinosaurs

In 1923, some scientists made a great discovery. They found unhatched fossil eggs buried in the desert. The eggs contained skeletons of baby Protoceratops. They were millions of years old. For the first time, it was known how dinosaurs were born. They were hatched from eggs just like other reptiles.

1. In which year did the scientists find the eggs?

    a. 1932    b. 1923    c. 1963

2. Fossil eggs were found

    _____ in the desert.
    (burst   buried   burned)

3. What word describes "a dry, sandy place"? _____

This is what the scientists learned: A mother Protoceratops laid her eggs in a "nest." The nest was in a sand dune beside a small pond. After the mother laid her eggs, she walked away and never came back. When born, baby Protoceratops looked exactly like their mother.

4. Write a word that means "next to": _____

5. How did baby Protoceratops look when they were born?

    _____

    _____

6. From the story you know that:
    a. Some Protoceratops never hatched.
    b. Dinosaurs are still alive.
    c. Protoceratops are the largest dinosaurs.

Name _____

## Brachiosaurus

Read the first sentence in each box. Decide what comes next. Find the correct sentence ending in the water below the Brachiosaurus and write it.

1. Brachiosaurus was the biggest of the big. It measured 85 feet

_____

_____ .

2. Brachiosaurus moved very slowly. It stayed in water, safe

_____

_____ .

3. This dinosaur weighed about 80 tons, which is as much as

_____

_____

a bird weighs

from unfriendly dinosaurs

from head to toe

16 large elephants weigh

run away too fast

**Brainwork:** Write three things you could do much better if your neck was as long as Brachiosaurus'.

88

## Tyrannosaurus Rex

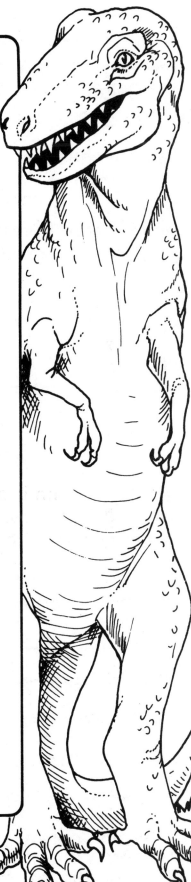

Tyrannosaurus Rex was called the "king of the tyrant lizards." It was the meanest of all the dinosaurs.

For such a huge dinosaur, TR (its nickname) could run very fast. Other dinosaurs were always on the lookout for TR. If TR was hungry, it would attack anything! Its teeth were six inches long and very sharp. TR also had sharp claws on the end of its short arms. **They** were used as "knives" to carve up food.

When TR was not looking for something to eat, it was sleeping. That is about all it did—eat and sleep.

1. In this story, "sharp" means:
   a. very smart
   b. pointed
   c. not cut

2. In the first paragraph, find a word that:

   a. names a kind of ruler _____

   b. is the opposite of "kindest"

   _____

3. The word "they" stands for:

   _____

4. Find and write a "measuring" word:

   _____

**Brainwork:** TR just ate and slept. What else do you think dinosaurs did during the day?

FS-32044 Reading

# Deinonychus

Do you know someone who has a bad temper? You probably stay out of the way when that person is around. Dinosaurs felt the same way about Deinonychus. This dinosaur was always feeling mean and angry. You can guess that Deinonychus did not have many good friends.

Deinonychus had very strong hands and feet and a big brain too. Deinonychus was about the size of a man. To other dinosaurs, it must have seemed to be 30 feet tall! Even the biggest dinosaurs were afraid of Deinonychus.

**Read each sentence. Choose the correct words to complete the sentence and write them.**

1. Deinonychus had a bad _____ .

   It _____ felt mean.

2. This dinosaur probably _____

   food from other _____ .

3. Deinonychus' _____ hands made

   it easy to grab an _____ .

4. Although only as _____ as a man,

   all other dinosaurs were _____ of it.

| |
|---|
| afraid |
| strong |
| tall |
| temper |
| stole |
| always |
| enemy |
| dinosaurs |

# Stegosaurus

1. Draw four plates on the Stegosaurus' neck...
2. Draw seven pairs of spines down its back. ...............
3. Draw a nail on each toe...
4. Draw four spikes on the tail..........
5. Draw three ferns along the water's edge.......

Name _____

# Pterodactylus

Read the story carefully. After 90 seconds, turn the paper over and answer the questions. Do not look back.

**1.**

Pterodactylus was about the size of a small robin.

**2.**

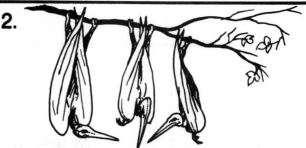

This flying reptile slept hanging upside down in trees.

**3.**

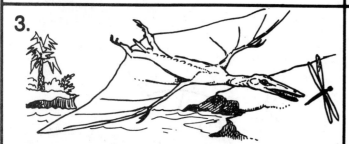

Pterodactylus lived near the water. It ate insects.

**4.**

It had a very long beak. The teeth were as sharp as needles.

✽ **NOTE: Fold here before giving to students (top half only showing).**

- - - - - - - - - - - - - - - - - - - - - - - - - - - - - - - - - - - - - - - -

## Answer in complete sentences.

1. How big was the Pterodactylus?

_____

2. Describe Pterodactylus' teeth.

_____

3. How did this reptile sleep?

_____

4. Where did Pterodactylus live?

_____

# Elephant Bird

The elephant bird was one of the largest birds ever to live. It was about eleven feet tall. Even though this bird had feathers, it could not fly.

Scientists have found huge fossil elephant bird eggshells. One shell could hold two gallons! Can you imagine eating an egg that big for breakfast?

There are many legends about the elephant bird. One story says that the bird could pick up an elephant in its claws and carry it away. (I thought the elephant bird couldn't fly, didn't you?)

**What comes before? What comes after? Complete each sentence. Read the story for clues.**

1. The elephant bird could not fly even though _____

_____.

2. _____ . Could you

eat an egg that big?

3. The elephant bird, one of the largest birds, was about _____

_____ .

4. A _____ is a story that is not always

true.

# Archaeopteryx

The next time you see a bird, look at it very carefully. Did you know that it is a real living relative of the dinosaur? Archaeopteryx is the first known bird that ever lived. It looked just like a small dinosaur except for one thing: feathers. This early bird was about the size of a crow. Most birds can fly, but the Archaeopteryx could not. It walked around on rocks or in tree branches.

Archaeopteryx was the first bird. Do you think birds will ever grow into huge dinosaurs like Tyrannosaurus Rex again? Tell why or why not. Write your answer on the back.

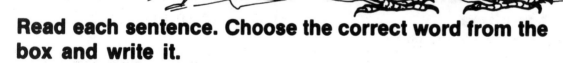

**Read each sentence. Choose the correct word from the box and write it.**

1. Archaeopteryx looked like a _____ dinosaur

   with _____ .

2. Scientists know Archaeopteryx could walk

   _____ they found its _____ .

3. Archaeopteryx was about the size of a

   _____ although it _____ not fly.

4. Archaeopteryx was the _____ bird ever

   to live on _____ .

first
crow
Earth
feathers
footprints
could
small
because

Name _____

## Elasmosaurus

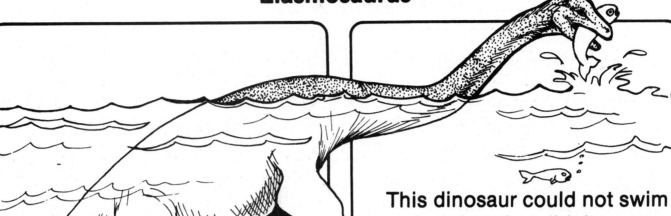

Elasmosaurus looked like a giant floating turtle. It would paddle along on top of the water looking for things to eat. Elasmosaurus was not a picky eater. It took a lot of food to fill up its huge stomach.

1. What did Elasmosaurus look

   like? _____

   _____

   _____

2. Find a sentence in the story that means the same as: "Elasmosaurus didn't have a favorite food."

   _____

   _____

This dinosaur could not swim very fast, but that didn't matter. It had such a long neck, it could easily snatch a fish swimming 20 feet away. Elasmosaurus used its flippers as oars to paddle around the ocean. Some scientists think this sea monster could "row" backwards as well as forwards.

3. Elasmosaurus could catch

   a fish swimming _____

   _____.

4. Find a word that is the opposite of "let go."

   _____

5. Another giant sea monster could easily catch Elasmosaurus.

   True     False

   Tell why or why not. Write your answer on the back.

FS-32044 Reading

Name _____

# Tylosaurus

If you had gone deep sea diving 70 million years ago, guess what would have been down there with you! A Tylosaurus, that's what.

This dinosaur looked like a crocodile, but it was as big as a great white shark! Its huge jaw and sharp teeth made it look even more fierce—especially when it was hungry!

**Answer the questions in complete sentences.**

1. What made the Tylosaurus look so fierce?

_____

_____

2. How long ago did the Tylosaurus live?

_____

_____

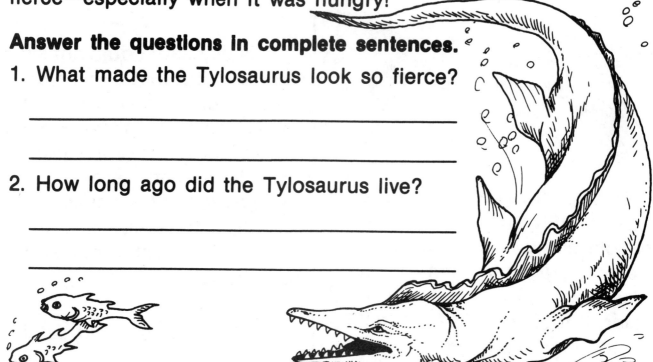

A long powerful tail helped the Tylosaurus swim at fast speeds. A slower moving sea monster would have had a hard time escaping the bite of the Tylosaurus. Can you imagine a fight between a Tylosaurus and an Elasmosaurus? The whipping and thrashing of tails would make it seem like a hurricane.

3. Why was the Tylosaurus so fast?

_____

4. What would a Tylosaurus and Elasmosaurus fight seem like?

_____

5. On the back, draw and color a sea monster that looks like: a whale, a lizard and a dolphin.

96                    FS-32044 Reading

# Dinohyus

After the dinosaurs became extinct, another kind of animal took their place. This animal, called a mammal, is still living today. (Bears, dogs, monkeys and human beings are all types of mammals.) Dinosaurs were not able to live in cold weather, but mammals can. Their fur or hair keeps them warm.

1. What happened to the dinosaurs? _____

_____

_____

2. Name 3 kinds of mammals.

_____

_____

_____

3. Find another word for "climate." Write it on the line.

_____

Dinohyus was a strange-looking mammal that lived about 40 million years ago. It had split hooves and two strong tusks just like pigs of today do. Large bones stuck out around the eyes. To make matters worse, its face looked like a baboon. When scientists found Dinohyus' skeletons, they noticed that many had broken bones. They probably broke their bones fighting enemies—and losing!

4. When did Dinohyus live?

_____

5. How did Dinohyus' face look?

_____

_____

6. In what way did Dinohyus look like a pig?

_____

_____

**Name** _____

# Ankylosaurus

Ankylosaurus looked like a "crawling tank." Its head and back were covered with plates of armor. Even the tail had heavy bones in it. The Ankylosaurus used its tail as a club. If an enemy got too close, Ankylosaurus would knock it flat. What a headache! Ankylosaurus had very tiny teeth and probably ate only soft plants.

**Answer the questions in complete sentences.**

1. How did Ankylosaurus use its tail?

_____

2. What did Ankylosaurus eat?

_____

3. What did an Ankylosaurus look like?

_____

4. What protected the Ankylosaurus' head? _____

_____

**Draw the Ankylosaurus. Give it something to eat.**

Name _____

## Antiarch

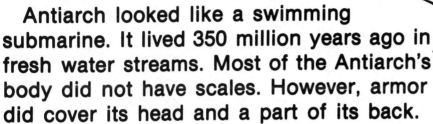

Antiarch looked like a swimming submarine. It lived 350 million years ago in fresh water streams. Most of the Antiarch's body did not have scales. However, armor did cover its head and a part of its back.

Do you see two strange looking "claws" near the Antiarch's head? This fish swam close to the bottom of a stream. Maybe the claws helped push Antiarch through plants and rocks. Antiarch ate small fish. How do you think it swallowed its food? Draw a picture on the back showing what Antiarch looked like without its face armor.

1. A good title for this story is:
   a. The Story of Armor
   b. A Strange Prehistoric Fish
   c. How Antiarch Swam

2. How long ago did Antiarch live?

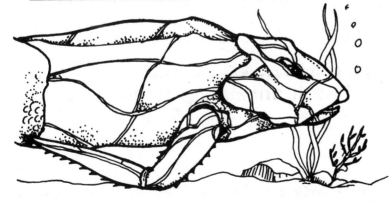

3. Where did Antiarch swim?

   _____

   _____

4. What did Antiarch look like?

   _____

   _____

5. "Scales" protect a fish. Write a different meaning for the word "scales."

   _____

   _____

**Brainwork:** Think of two reasons why Antiarch had those "claws." Answer in a complete sentence.

_____

_____

99

Name _____

## Brontosaurus

The first human had not yet been born 65 million years ago. How then do we know that dinosaurs really existed? Read the story under each picture to find out.

**1.** 130 million years ago...

The Brontosaurus dies in the forest.

**2.**

Its skin rots. The bones are covered with dirt carried by the wind.

**3.**

Thousands of years later, the dirt and bones turn into stone.

**4.**

Brontosaurus remains hidden for millions of years.

**5.**

Heavy rains beat against the mountain. The rock wears away.

**6.** 100 years ago...

A scientist finds Brontosaurus' bones. These bones are called fossils.

1. Write a word that means the same as "rock." _____

2. The Brontosaurus was hidden for _____ of years.

   It was buried under a _____ .

3. **Fact** or **Opinion**? The scientist was very excited when he discovered

   the fossils. _____

**Brainwork:** What do you think animals will look like in 30 million years? Write three sentences on the back. Draw a picture.

       FS-32044 Reading

# Dinosaur Tales

Read the clues about each dinosaur. Find the correct matching picture.
Write the dinosaur's name on the line.

1. **Triceratops**—It had three horns on its head. Its mouth was shaped like a beak.

2. **Corythosaurus**—This dinosaur had a head shaped like a helmet. Its "hands" were webbed like the feet of a duck.

3. **Diplodocus**—This was the longest dinosaur. It was 90 feet from head to tail.

4. **Tyrannosaurus Rex** was a very fierce dinosaur. Its teeth were six inches long! Its arms were very short.

5. **Ankylosaurus**—This dinosaur looked like a "walking tank." Its tail looked like a club.

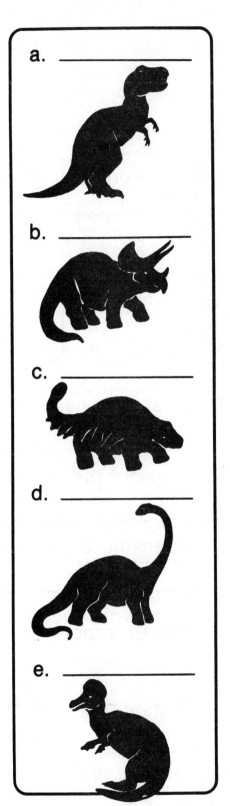

a. _____

b. _____

c. _____

d. _____

e. _____

FS-32044 Reading

# Where Did They Go?

What ever happened to the dinosaurs? About 65 million years ago, they became extinct. Scientists are not sure, but they think perhaps:

a) A huge star crashed into Earth, making it as hot as an oven. The heat may have killed the plants that dinosaurs ate.

b) Dinosaurs could live only in a warm climate. Over the years, the weather cooled down. Dinosaurs could not keep warm. Can you imagine a Brontosaurus trying to curl up in a cave?

Dinosaurs ruled the earth for about 140 million years. Scientists are still finding their fossils. Who knows what other amazing secrets may still be hidden beneath the earth?

1. What may have killed the plants?

_____

2. How did the weather change?

_____

3. When did dinosaurs become extinct?

_____

4. What word means the same as "died out"?

_____

5. Why couldn't dinosaurs live in cold weather?

_____

**Brainwork:** Pretend you have a pet dinosaur. What would you do to keep it warm in winter?

 FS-32044 Reading

## Finding Fossils

Let's go on a fossil hunt. Cut out the sentences. Look at each picture carefully. Decide which sentence best fits the picture. Paste it in the box.

**c.** All ready. These fossils are ready to go to the museum.

**f.** Let's put up a tent and start looking for more bones.

**b.** Look! I think I've found a fossil.

**e.** Wow! This dinosaur was huge. Take pictures.

**a.** I'll put a number on all these bones before packing them.

**d.** Be careful! It's easy to shatter those bones.

FS-32044 Reading

# Make a Fossil!

Making your own fossil is easy and fun. All you need is plaster of Paris, clay, a narrow piece of tagboard and a leaf (or shell).

**1.**

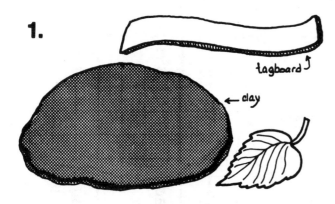

Flatten the clay (¾" thickness) into a circle larger than the leaf.

**2.**

Make a ring out of the tagboard and press it into the clay. Press the leaf into the clay. Make it lie flat.

**3.**

Mix plaster of Paris with water until it turns to a thin paste. Pour over the leaf (about ½") and let it set.

**4.**

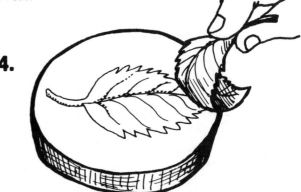

When the plaster has hardened, remove the ring and peel away the clay. Peel the leaf off— gently! Now you have a fossil!

**Write these sentences in order as they happened in the story.**

Peel off the leaf.              1. _____

Press leaf into the clay.       2. _____

Flatten the clay.               3. _____

Mix plaster of Paris.           4. _____

FS-32044 Reading

# Answer Key

---

**Name** _____

**Read the story.**
Let's learn how to mix paint. You can make a new color. Get a small dish. Put some yellow paint in the dish. Add a little bit of blue paint. Now stir to mix the new color. You made green paint.

**Read the sentences in the box below. Write them in order as they happened in the story.**

**1** Get a dish.

**2** Put the yellow paint in the dish.

**3** Add some blue paint.

**4** Stir the paint.

**5** Look at the green paint.

| Put the yellow paint in the dish. |
| Stir the paint. |
| Look at the green paint. |
| Get a dish. |
| Add some blue paint. |

**Draw a line under the best ending for the story.**

You can eat lunch.
You can paint a tree.
You have three new colors.

Page 1

---

**Name** _____

**Read the story.**
Every morning I must get ready for school. I do not want to miss the bus. After breakfast I put my books in my book bag. Then I put on my coat and walk to the bus stop. I wait for the bus with my friends. The bus comes at eight o'clock.

**Read the sentences in the box below. Write them in order as they happened in the story.**

**1** I eat breakfast.

**2** I put my books in my bag.

**3** I put on my coat.

**4** I go to the bus stop.

**5** I wait for the bus.

| I go to the bus stop. |
| I put my books in my bag. |
| I eat breakfast. |
| I put on my coat. |
| I wait for the bus. |

**Draw a line under the best ending for the story.**

I will walk to school.
I ride the bus to the store.
I ride the bus to school.

Page 2

---

**Name** _____

**Read the story.**
Dad and I went to the park. We were going to rent a boat for an hour. Dad paid for the boat. I got into the boat. Dad climbed in. We rowed around the pond. I learned to steer and row the boat.

**Read the sentences in the box below. Write them in order as they happened in the story.**

**1** We went to the park.

**2** Dad paid for the boat.

**3** I climbed into the boat.

**4** Dad got in the boat.

**5** We rowed around the pond.

| I climbed into the boat. |
| We rowed around the pond. |
| Dad paid for the boat. |
| Dad got in the boat. |
| We went to the park. |

**Draw a line under the best ending for the story.**

We rowed out to the ocean.
We took the boat back to the dock.
We took the boat home.

Page 3

---

**Name** _____

**Read the story.**
Tomorrow is my friend's birthday party. I bought a book for her. I put a picture of myself inside the book cover. I put the book in a box. I wrapped the box in pink and yellow paper. I wrote, "Happy Birthday to Jan—from Kim".

**Read the sentences in the box below. Write them in order as they happened in the story.**

**1** I bought a book.

**2** I put my picture in the book.

**3** I put it in a box.

**4** I wrapped the gift.

**5** I wrote a note.

| I bought a book. |
| I wrapped the gift. |
| I put it in a box. |
| I wrote a note. |
| I put my picture in the book. |

**Draw a line under the best ending for the story.**

Kim keeps the book.
Kim mails the gift to Jim
Kim goes to Jan's party.

Page 4

---

    FS-32044 Reading

# Answer Key

**Read the story.**

I need to talk to Ted. I looked up his telephone number and called his house. His mother said, "Call back after five o'clock." I will call Ted again just before dinner. He will be home then.

**Read the sentences in the box below. Write them in order as they happened in the story.**

**1** I looked up Ted's number.

**2** I called his house.

**3** I talked to his mother.

**4** She said, "Ted is not home."

**5** She asked me to call later.

| She said, "Ted is not home." |
| I looked up Ted's number. |
| I talked to his mother. |
| I called his house. |
| She asked me to call later. |

**Draw a line under the best ending for the story.**

Ted will call me.
I talk to Jack on the telephone.
I will call again and talk to Ted.

Page 5

---

**Read the story.**

Meg was on the swing. She said, "Watch me!" She jumped off while she was still swinging. Meg fell down and hurt her leg. She cried. She walked to the office. Meg told the nurse about her leg.

**Read the sentences in the box below. Write them in order as they happened in the story.**

**1** Meg was swinging.

**2** Meg said, "Watch me!"

**3** Meg jumped from the swing.

**4** Meg cried.

**5** Meg walked to the office.

| Meg jumped from the swing. |
| Meg was swinging. |
| Meg cried. |
| Meg walked to the office. |
| Meg said, "Watch me!" |

**Draw a line under the best ending for the story.**

Meg said, "This is fun."
The school nurse will help Meg.
Meg lost her shoe.

Page 6

---

**Read the story.**

My grandmother gave me a new game. I asked my sister to play the game with me. The doorbell rang. It was my friend Don. He played the game with us. Mother wants to play the game after dinner. That will be fun!

**Read the sentences in the box below. Write them in order as they happened in the story.**

**1** I have a new game.

**2** I asked my sister to play.

**3** Someone was at the door.

**4** Don played with us.

**5** Mother wants to play later.

| Don played with us. |
| I asked my sister to play. |
| Mother wants to play later. |
| I have a new game. |
| Someone was at the door. |

**Draw a line under the best ending for the story.**

Mother can't find the game.
Don took the game home.
I wrote a thank you note to Grandmother.

Page 7

---

**Read the story.**

The traffic light is broken. A policewoman is telling the cars when to go. Two men came in a yellow truck to fix the light. Their truck had a ladder on it. One man climbed up and fixed the light. The policewoman and workmen left.

**Read the sentences in the box below. Write them in order as they happened in the story.**

**1** She told the cars when to go.

**2** A yellow truck came.

**3** Two men worked on the light.

**4** The workmen fixed the light.

**5** The workmen went away.

| The workmen fixed the light. |
| A yellow truck came. |
| She told the cars when to go. |
| Two men worked on the light. |
| The workmen went away. |

**Draw a line under the best ending for the story.**

Now the light is working fine.
They took the light down.
They put in a stop sign.

Page 8

---

# Answer Key

---

Name _____

**Read the story.**

On Saturdays Dad and I clean up our yard. I rake the leaves. Dad pulls the weeds while I cut the grass. Then we sweep the sidewalk. We water the plants if it has not rained during the week. If it rains on Saturday and Sunday we do not do yard work.

**Read the sentences in the box below. Write them in order as they happened in the story.**

**1** Dad and I go outside.

**2** I rake the leaves.

**3** I cut the grass.

**4** We sweep the sidewalk.

**5** We water the plants.

| We water the plants. |
| Dad and I go outside. |
| I rake the leaves. |
| I cut the grass. |
| We sweep the sidewalk. |

**Draw a line under the best ending for the story.**

Dad digs a big hole in the grass.
<u>Mother says, "The yard looks nice."</u>
Mother says, "Our yard looks dirty."

Page 9

---

Name _____

**Read the story.**

I wanted a pet bird so I bought a cage. I saved money to buy the bird. Before school I give him food and water. I put clean paper on the bottom of the cage. Before I go to bed I cover his cage with a blanket. Then he is warm at night.

**Read the sentences in the box below. Write them in order as they happened in the story.**

**1** I bought a cage.

**2** I bought a bird.

**3** I feed my bird.

**4** I put paper in his cage.

**5** I put a blanket over the cage.

| I feed my bird. |
| I bought a bird. |
| I put paper in his cage. |
| I bought a cage. |
| I put a blanket over the cage. |

**Draw a line under the best ending for the story.**

The bird flies to the top of the tree.
<u>The bird goes to sleep.</u>
The bird is my brother's pet.

Page 10

---

Name _____

**Read the story.**

I must unlock my bike and I can't find the key anywhere. Will you help me? It is a silver key. Please look in my room. I'll go ask my mother if she has seen it. It may be in the pocket of my other pants.

**Read the sentences in the box below. Write them in order as they happened in the story.**

**1** I must unlock my bike.

**2** My key is lost.

**3** Look for the key in my room.

**4** I will ask Mother.

**5** Maybe it's in my other pants.

| I must unlock my bike. |
| I will ask Mother. |
| Look for the key in my room. |
| Maybe it's in my other pants. |
| My key is lost. |

**Draw a line under the best ending for the story.**

<u>I found the key in my pants pocket.</u>
I found the missing bike.
I do not need a key.

Page 11

---

Name _____

**Read the story.**

Tom is getting ready for a camping trip. His flashlight will not work. The light bulb is broken. At the store he found the bulb he needed. He bought the bulb and put it in. Now the flashlight works again.

**Read the sentences in the box below. Write them in order as they happened in the story.**

**1** The flashlight needs a bulb.

**2** Tom went to the store.

**3** He found the bulb.

**4** He put in the light bulb.

**5** Now the flashlight works.

| The flashlight needs a bulb. |
| Now the flashlight works. |
| He put in the light bulb. |
| Tom went to the store. |
| He found the bulb. |

**Draw a line under the best ending for the story.**

The flashlight will not work.
Tom hides the flashlight.
<u>Tom takes the flashlight with him.</u>

Page 12

---

FS-32044 Reading

# Answer Key

Name

**Read the story.**

Our neighbors are away on vacation. Mr. Jones asked me to take care of their home. I must feed their cat. I pick up the mail. After school I get the paper from the driveway. They will pay me for taking good care of their home.

**Read the sentences in the box below. Write them in order as they happened in the story.**

**1** Mr. Jones asked me to help.

**2** I feed the cat.

**3** I take care of the mail.

**4** I pick up the paper.

**5** I will be paid.

| |
|---|
| I feed the cat. |
| I take care of the mail. |
| Mr. Jones asked me to help. |
| I will be paid. |
| I pick up the paper. |

**Draw a line under the best ending for the story.**

Mr. Jones is angry.
Mr. Jones pays me for doing a good job.
Mr. Jones does not care about his house.

Page 13

---

Name

**Read the story.**

We have a special reading time at school. Everyone picks a book to read. I have my own quiet reading time at home now. At bedtime I get ready and then I look at the clock. I read for fifteen minutes. Then I turn out the light. My reading time at home adds up to 105 minutes each week.

**Read the sentences in the box below. Write them in order as they happened in the story.**

**1** We have reading at school.

**2** I have reading time at home.

**3** I get ready for bed.

**4** I read for fifteen minutes.

**5** I turn out the light.

| |
|---|
| I get ready for bed. |
| We have reading at school. |
| I have reading time at home. |
| I turn out the light. |
| I read for fifteen minutes. |

**Draw a line under the best ending for the story.**

I cannot find my book.
I read many books.
I do not have a library card.

Page 14

---

Name

**Read the story.**

My dance class is on Thursdays. I bring my tap shoes to school. I go to dance class on the bus after school. I put on my tap shoes. Then I take my lesson. After class my brother takes me home.

**Read the sentences in the box below. Write them in order as they happened in the story.**

**1** I take my dancing shoes to school.

**2** I ride the bus to dancing school.

**3** I put on my tap shoes.

**4** My dancing lesson begins.

**5** My brother takes me home.

| |
|---|
| I ride the bus to dancing school. |
| I put on my tap shoes. |
| I take my dancing shoes to school. |
| My brother takes me home. |
| My dancing lesson begins. |

**Draw a line under the best ending for the story.**

I practice tap dancing at home.
I only dance on Thursdays.
I must get new shoes.

Page 15

---

Name

**Read the story.**

I started a club. I asked a few friends to join. Five of my friends said yes. We had our first club meeting. We have a name for our club—THE SUPER KIDS. We will have a campout in Jim's yard.

**Read the sentences in the box below. Write them in order as they happened in the story.**

**1** I wanted to start a club.

**2** I asked some friends to join.

**3** Five people joined my club.

**4** We had our first meeting.

**5** We plan to have a campout.

| |
|---|
| We had our first meeting. |
| Five people joined my club. |
| I asked some friends to join. |
| We plan to have a campout. |
| I wanted to start a club. |

**Draw a line under the best ending for the story.**

It is hard to start a club.
It costs too much money to have a club.
The campout is fun for everyone.

Page 16

# Answer Key

---

Name _____

**Read the story.**
I made a book about football. On the cover I wrote the names of football players. I found pictures and stories about football. I cut them out and pasted them in my book. On Friday it will be my turn to share at school. I will share my football book.

**Read the sentences in the box below. Write them in order as they happened in the story.**

**1** I made a book.

**2** I wrote names on the cover.

**3** I cut out pictures and stories.

**4** I pasted pictures in my book.

**5** I will take it to school.

| I wrote names on the cover. |
| I made a book. |
| I cut out pictures and stories. |
| I will take it to school. |
| I pasted pictures in my book. |

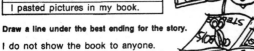

**Draw a line under the best ending for the story.**

I do not show the book to anyone.
I show the book to my class on Friday.
I took the book back to the library.

Page 17

---

Name _____

**Read the story.**
My brother is having a birthday party. His friends will come. They will play lots of games. Mom made a big cake. We set the table. We have party hats for everyone. Dad and I blew up balloons. We are ready to begin.

**Read the sentences in the box below. Write them in order as they happened in the story.**

**1** There is going to be a party.

**2** A big cake is made.

**3** Everyone will have a hat.

**4** We blew up balloons.

**5** Everything is ready.

| A big cake is made. |
| We blew up balloons. |
| There is going to be a party. |
| Everything is ready. |
| Everyone will have a hat. |

**Draw a line under the best ending for the story.**

We must buy a cake.
The Christmas party is fun.
The doorbell rings and everyone comes in.

Page 18

---

Name _____

**Read the story.**
Let's go fishing. Put a piece of bait on the hook. Throw your line in the water. Watch the float. When it moves up and down a fish is eating the bait. Pull up the rod and wind it in. Maybe you will have a fish.

**Read the sentences in the box below. Write them in order as they happened in the story.**

**1** Let's go fishing.

**2** First you must bait your hook.

**3** Put the line in the water.

**4** Watch the float carefully.

**5** Pull in the fish.

| First you must bait your hook. |
| Put the line in the water. |
| Let's go fishing. |
| Watch the float carefully. |
| Pull in the fish. |

**Draw a line under the best ending for the story.**

You can eat the fish for dinner.
There are no fish in the lake.
I am afraid of turtles.

Page 19

---

Name _____

**Read the story.**
Our shoe store is having a sale. Dad and I went to the store. I tried on a pair of blue shoes. They were too small. I tried on some brown shoes. I wanted blue in a bigger size. We bought bigger blue shoes.

**Read the sentences in the box below. Write them in order as they happened in the story.**

**1** Shoes are on sale.

**2** We went to the shoe store.

**3** I tried on small shoes.

**4** I tried on brown shoes.

**5** I bought blue shoes.

| We went to the shoe store. |
| Shoes are on sale. |
| I tried on small shoes. |
| I bought blue shoes. |
| I tried on brown shoes. |

**Draw a line under the best ending for the story.**

I wore the blue shoes to school.
Dad wore the new shoes to work.
We bought two pairs of shoes.

Page 20

---

# Answer Key

---

## Page 21

Name _____

Dear Donna,

I would like you to come to a party at my house next Saturday. It is going to be a surprise birthday party for Judy.

We are going to have hot dogs and chips for lunch. My mother has bought some new games for us to play. Then we will light seven candles on the cake for Judy to blow out. We'll have ice cream to eat too, and something cold to drink. At 3 o'clock my mother is going to take us to the show to see "Cricket Goes to Washington". I hope you can come.

Be sure to be here before 12 o'clock.

Love,
Molly

1. A good name for this story would be:
   a. Going to the Show
   **b. A Surprise Party**
   c. Eating Cake and Ice Cream

2. Molly is writing a ___letter___ to Donna.
   a. test
   **b. letter**
   c. paper

3. Who is going to be seven years old?
   a. Molly
   b. Nancy
   **c. Judy**

4. What word in the story means "to wish"?
   **a. hope**
   b. lost
   c. eat

5. How do you think Judy will feel when she comes to Molly's house?
   **a. happy**
   b. sad
   c. angry

Page 21

---

## Page 22

Name _____

"I am a blue bird. Green trees are nice and red flowers are pretty, but I think they would look better if they were blue like me. I'll ask Homer if I can use some of his blue paint tonight."

"Help yourself, Blue Bird," Homer said, hopping around his cage. "But be sure to bring it back. I have to paint my Easter eggs soon."

Blue Bird flew from tree to tree painting everything blue. The next morning all the neighbors came outside. "What has happened? All the colors are gone! Blue is such a sad color." And they all began to cry.

"I guess not everyone likes blue the best. I'll wash all the trees and flowers tonight and then they will all be happy again."

1. A good name for this story would be:
   **a. A Bird That Likes Blue**
   b. Painting at Night
   c. Coloring trees and Flowers

2. Homer wanted Blue Bird to ___return___ his paints.
   a. throw away
   b. drink
   **c. return**

3. Where did Blue Bird do most of his painting?
   a. under the houses
   **b. in the gardens**
   c. in Homer's cage

4. What word in the story means "unhappy"?
   a. best
   **b. sad**
   c. soon

5. Homer has to paint his eggs soon. What do you think Homer is?
   a. a dog
   **b. a rabbit**
   c. a chicken

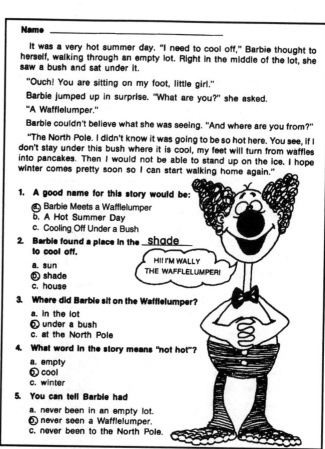

Page 22

---

## Page 23

Name _____

The mother hen sat on her eggs all night. Early the next morning, one egg popped open and out jumped a mouse. "What are you doing here? You're not one of my babies!" cried the hen.

"I don't have a mother to take care of me," the little mouse answered. "But if you will help me, I can look like one of your babies." One by one, the mouse brought some feathers to the mother hen. "Stick these on my back. Now, don't I look soft and furry?"

Just then, a little chicken walked over. "Do you want to go out and play with me?"

"Squeak, squeak, squeak," the mouse said.

"Oh, no," sighed the mother hen. "Now what do I do with you?"

1. A good name for this story would be:
   **a. Mother Hen's New Baby**
   b. A Duck Goes Out to Play
   c. Animals in the Barn

2. "I don't have a mother. Can I be your ___baby___ ?"
   a. chicken
   **b. baby**
   c. mouse

3. When did mother hen sit on her eggs?
   a. in the morning
   **b. at night**
   c. before lunch

4. What word in the story means the opposite of "late"?
   ___early___

5. What do you think the mother hen will do next?
   a. teach the mouse to quack
   b. teach the mouse to meow
   **c. teach the mouse to cluck**

Page 23

---

## Page 24

Name _____

It was a very hot summer day. "I need to cool off," Barbie thought to herself, walking through an empty lot. Right in the middle of the lot, she saw a bush and sat under it.

"Ouch! You are sitting on my foot, little girl."

Barbie jumped up in surprise. "What are you?" she asked.

"A Wafflelumper."

Barbie couldn't believe what she was seeing. "And where are you from?"

"The North Pole. I didn't know it was going to be so hot here. You see, if I don't stay under this bush where it is cool, my feet will turn from waffles into pancakes. Then I would not be able to stand up on the ice. I hope winter comes pretty soon so I can start walking home again."

1. A good name for this story would be:
   **a. Barbie Meets a Wafflelumper**
   b. A Hot Summer Day
   c. Cooling Off Under a Bush

2. Barbie found a place in the ___shade___ to cool off.
   a. sun
   **b. shade**
   c. house

3. Where did Barbie sit on the Wafflelumper?
   a. in the lot
   **b. under a bush**
   c. at the North Pole

4. What word in the story means "not hot"?
   a. empty
   **b. cool**
   c. winter

5. You can tell Barbie had
   a. never been in an empty lot.
   **b. never seen a Wafflelumper.**
   c. never been to the North Pole.

HI! I'M WALLY THE WAFFLELUMPER!

Page 24

---

110

# Answer Key

Adam hopped out of bed early Sunday morning just as the sun was coming up. "I hope the Easter Bunny left me lots of eggs and some candy." He looked all around. He hunted and hunted but couldn't find one egg. When he looked behind the last big bush in his yard, Adam saw something that made his hair stand on end.

"What are you doing here, Santa Claus? This is Easter, not Christmas!"

"The Easter Bunny is sick today and he gave me this basket to take around to all the houses. But he didn't tell me where to leave these eggs."

"I'll show you what to do, Santa Claus." They hopped off down the street, hiding eggs in the grass and under the flowers.

1. A good name for this story would be:
   a. A Christmas Story
   (b.) Santa Claus Finds a Helper
   c. The Easter Bunny Brings Some Eggs

2. Adam looked all around his __garden__ for eggs.
   a. house
   (b.) garden
   c. room

3. What did the Easter Bunny want Santa Claus to do?
   (a.) hide the eggs and candy
   b. wait for him at Adam's house
   c. color all the eggs yellow

4. What word means the same thing as "looked for"?
   a. left
   b. hopped
   (c.) hunted

5. Santa Claus felt glad when he found someone to
   (a.) help him.
   b. feed him.
   c. talk to him.

Page 25

---

"Michelle, why are you still awake?" Mother asked, sitting on the bed. "It's after 10 o'clock."

"I'm waiting for the airplane. After I go to sleep tonight, I thought I might like to take a trip to Terry's house. I read about her in a book today. She lives far away in a place called Hawaii. Every day Terry and her friends go swimming, take a boat ride and play in the sand. Then maybe someday, when Terry is sound asleep, she can fly over here to our house and I'll show her how to build a snowman."

"I hope you have a good time tonight, Michelle," Mother said, "but be sure to be back at 7 in the morning so you will get to school on time."

1. A good name for this story would be:
   a. Playing By the Sea
   b. Going to School
   (c.) Dreaming About a Trip

2. Michelle had to fall __asleep__ before taking a trip.
   a. down
   b. awake
   (c.) asleep

3. What was Michelle going to do in Hawaii?
   a. work and read
   (b.) swim and play
   c. write and ride

4. Which word reminds you of the ocean?
   a. ride
   (b.) sand
   c. school

5. Michelle did not really go to Hawaii. She was only
   a. thinking.
   (b.) dreaming.
   c. playing.

Page 26

---

My mother left town this morning to go and visit my grandfather and she won't be back for two days. Tonight my Dad fixed dinner for my sister and me. He stayed in the kitchen for a long time. I thought he was making enough food to last for both days. When Dad called us to the table, I was a little surprised. It looked very different from what mother cooks for dinner. Here is what we had:

   4 pieces of bread (a little burned), peanut butter (no jelly), spaghetti (with hot dogs on top), popcorn (no butter)

"This looks really good!" Marla said. "Don't you think so, Jeff? I sure hope Mom stays at grandfather's for two or three weeks so you can cook for us all the time, Dad."

1. A good name for this story would be:
   (a.) Dad Takes Over in the Kitchen
   b. Mother Goes to Grandfather's
   c. Dad Burns the Dinner

2. Marla wanted Dad to fix dinner __every night__.
   a. one night
   (b.) every night
   c. in the morning

3. What did Dad cook for dinner?
   a. eggs
   b. bananas
   (c.) popcorn

4. What word means "not the same"?
   a. burned
   (b.) different
   c. enough

5. You might think that Dad
   a. was too tired to cook.
   (b.) had never cooked dinner before.
   c. did not like meat.

Page 27

---

"Who spilled this milk all over the kitchen floor?" Mother shouted. "Do you know who did this, Marty?"

"My hand did it. I told it to be careful, but it went ahead and dropped the bottle anyway. That was my right hand. This morning, my left hand broke your best dish in the backyard. The pieces flew everywhere! While I was cleaning up the dish, both of my feet stepped into your flower garden. I said, 'Watch out, feet!' but it was too late. There are no flowers anymore."

"I think I better take you to the doctor and have him give you some new hands and feet," Mother said.

"Wait a minute, Mother. From now on, I'll tell my hands and feet to be careful and stay out of trouble."

1. A good name for this story would be:
   (a.) Hands and Feet in Trouble
   b. Cleaning Up the House
   c. Going to the Doctor

2. Marty __talked__ to his feet in the garden.
   a. barked
   b. quacked
   (c.) talked

3. What did Marty drop with his right hand?
   a. flowers
   (b.) milk
   c. pieces

4. What word in the story means "not early"?
   a. broke
   b. minute
   (c.) late

5. Marty's hands and feet would not
   a. clean up the floor.
   (b.) do what he told them to.
   c. go to the store.

Page 28

# Answer Key

I have a face, but no mouth, no eyes and no nose. I have two **hands** and sometimes even three. You need me to tell you when to go to bed and when to get up. I sometimes make a loud buzzing sound to wake you up at dawn.

You can hang me on the wall or put me on the table. If I am very big, people call me "grandfather". One time, a mouse ran up me and then back down again. I cannot talk, but I can tick.

Can you tell me what I am?

1. A good name for this story would be:

   a. Time to Get Up
   ⓑ Guess What I Am?
   c. Learning to Tell Time

2. If you don't have a clock, a __watch__ can tell the time.

   ⓐ watch
   b. record
   c. dancer

3. What do the **hands** in this story do?

   a. clean the face of the clock
   ⓑ tell the time of day
   c. point to letters on the clock

4. What word in the story means "early in morning"?
   __dawn__

5. If a clock says 6 o'clock, it could be time for

   ⓐ dinner.
   b. school.
   c. lunch.

Page 29

---

"I wish I could be someone's pet, but nobody seems to want a rat around the house. Maybe if I went down to the pet shop, Mr. Sam would put me in his window where all the children would notice me. This weekend, I'll learn how to roll over like a dog, purr like a cat and sing like a bird."

Monday morning, the little rat skipped over to the pet store, bounced up on Mr. Sam's lap and meowed as soft as he could.

"You can't fool me," said Mr. Sam. "I know a rat when I see one. Don't be sad because you can't be a pet. We need good rats like you to eat up all the bad spiders and bugs in the city that might hurt people. If you work hard, I'll write a story about you in the Animal Book called: 'OUR HERO, THE RAT.'"

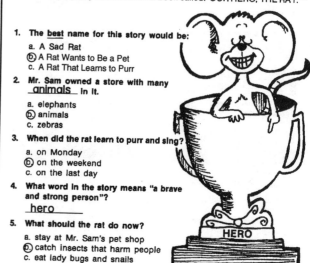

1. The **best** name for this story would be:

   a. A Sad Rat
   ⓑ A Rat Wants to Be a Pet
   c. A Rat That Learns to Purr

2. Mr. Sam owned a store with many __animals__ in it.

   a. elephants
   ⓑ animals
   c. zebras

3. When did the rat learn to purr and sing?

   a. on Monday
   ⓑ on the weekend
   c. on the last day

4. What word in the story means "a brave and strong person"?
   __hero__

5. What should the rat do now?

   a. stay at Mr. Sam's pet shop
   ⓑ catch insects that harm people
   c. eat lady bugs and snails

Page 30

---

"I'm going to build my own house right here in this tree. It will be just for my friends and me. We can eat cookies and drink milk up here."

"That sounds like a good idea,"Mother told Millie. "I'll get you a **saw** and some wood and nails to use when you are building your house."

Millie climbed up the tree and worked very hard all afternoon. She sawed away some branches to make room for the kitchen and a window too. Soon she was all finished.

"Mother, I can't get down," Millie shouted. "I cut off too many branches and now I'm stuck up here in this tree."

1. The **best** name for this story would be:

   ⓐ Millie Builds a Tree House
   b. Building With Nails and Wood
   c. A Tree House for Friends

2. Millie will need to get a __ladder__ to get down.

   a. chair
   ⓑ ladder
   c. swing

3. Millie needed three things to build with:

   a. a saw, nails and branches
   b. a tree, wood and nails
   ⓒ a saw, wood and nails

4. The word **saw** in this story means:

   a. to see someone
   ⓑ a tool to cut with
   c. something to climb on

5. You can tell that Millie did not

   a. want to build a tree house.
   ⓑ plan ahead before sawing.
   c. know how to climb a tree.

Page 31

---

I look just like my brother and he looks very much like me. My mother gets mixed up sometimes and calls me John instead of Jim. I don't mind, though, except when John gets into trouble and I get sent to my room by mistake. We can share our clothes and shoes because we are both the same size and shape.

Most people can't tell us apart. We like to fool the teacher by answering questions at the same time and changing chairs when she is not looking. All our friends call us John-Jim and Jim-John. They can never tell which is which. John and I have a secret that no one has discovered yet.

John can whistle, but I can't!

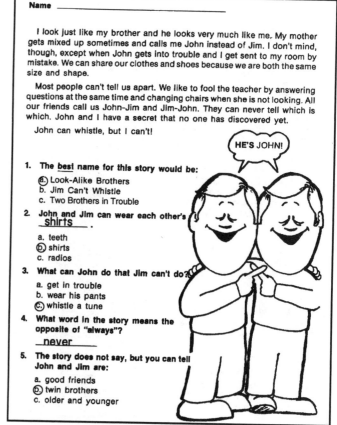

1. The **best** name for this story would be:

   ⓐ Look-Alike Brothers
   b. Jim Can't Whistle
   c. Two Brothers in Trouble

2. John and Jim can wear each other's __shirts__.

   a. teeth
   ⓑ shirts
   c. radios

3. What can John do that Jim can't do?

   a. get in trouble
   b. wear his pants
   ⓒ whistle a tune

4. What word in the story means the opposite of "always"?
   __never__

5. The story does not say, but you can tell John and Jim are:

   a. good friends
   ⓑ twin brothers
   c. older and younger

Page 32

# Answer Key

Name _____

Father stood in the doorway and watched Toby pack his clothes in a bag. "Where are you going, Toby?"

"I'm leaving home, Dad. I'm taking my bike and riding far away. I'm kind of tired of cleaning my room and washing dishes. I just want to ride and play from now on."

"I'm sorry you will have to leave so soon. Who will go to the ocean with me this summer?" asked Father. "What will I do with this new kite I bought? I guess I'll just have to get myself another son."

Toby sat down and thought a minute. "Maybe I could stay for one more day if you need someone to help you fly that kite."

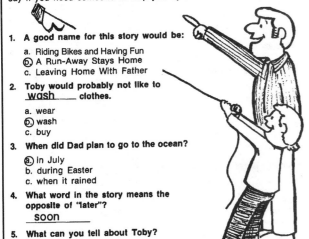

1. **A good name for this story would be:**
   a. Riding Bikes and Having Fun
   b. A Run-Away Stays Home
   c. Leaving Home With Father

2. **Toby would probably not like to** __wash__ **clothes.**
   a. wear
   b. wash
   c. buy

3. **When did Dad plan to go to the ocean?**
   a. in July
   b. during Easter
   c. when it rained

4. **What word in the story means the opposite of "later"?**
   __soon__

5. **What can you tell about Toby?**
   a. He didn't really want to leave home.
   b. He didn't know how to pack his clothes.
   c. He didn't know where to run away to.

Page 33

---

Name _____

"Eat your carrots, Debbie," Mother said leaving the kitchen. "Vegetables are good for you. Remember, no ice cream until you finish."

"Blah! I could get sick if I eat these." Just as Debbie was about to take her first bite, she felt a tail rub against her leg. "Rufus! You're just in time," she whispered. "Have a carrot." Debbie fed her dog four more carrots and then told him to go out the back door. "All finished, Mom. Come look."

"Open your mouth, Debbie. I want to see if you are hiding any in there." Debbie opened wide. "Debbie Teasdale, what have you done with those carrots? If you really ate your carrots, your teeth would be orange, but yours are as white as can be!"

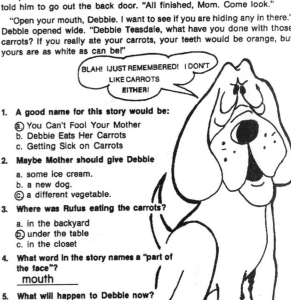

BLAH! I JUST REMEMBERED! I DON'T LIKE CARROTS EITHER!

1. **A good name for this story would be:**
   a. You Can't Fool Your Mother
   b. Debbie Eats Her Carrots
   c. Getting Sick on Carrots

2. **Maybe Mother should give Debbie**
   a. some ice cream.
   b. a new dog.
   c. a different vegetable.

3. **Where was Rufus eating the carrots?**
   a. in the backyard
   b. under the table
   c. in the closet

4. **What word in the story names a "part of the face"?**
   __mouth__

5. **What will happen to Debbie now?**
   a. She will have to go to bed.
   b. Mother will give her some bread.
   c. She cannot have anything to eat after dinner.

Page 34

---

Name _____

While walking home one evening by moonlight, I had the feeling someone was following me. I stopped a minute to listen and then said to myself, "You had better start running, Tommy, before he catches up to you." I squeezed under a fence and took a shortcut through Mr. Gumper's backyard. But I knew he was still there, only a few feet away.

I raced home as fast as I could and locked the front door. As soon as I turned on the light, there he was again, standing by the wall.

When I woke up the next morning, there wasn't a sign of my follower anywhere, although I know he will be back again tonight to follow me around by the moonlight. I'm not afraid because he has been walking behind me for almost nine years. We are good friends, my shadow and me.

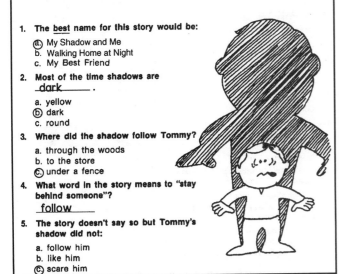

1. **The best name for this story would be:**
   a. My Shadow and Me
   b. Walking Home at Night
   c. My Best Friend

2. **Most of the time shadows are** __dark__ .
   a. yellow
   b. dark
   c. round

3. **Where did the shadow follow Tommy?**
   a. through the woods
   b. to the store
   c. under a fence

4. **What word in the story means to "stay behind someone"?**
   __follow__

5. **The story doesn't say so but Tommy's shadow did not:**
   a. follow him
   b. like him
   c. scare him

Page 35

---

Name _____

Once, many years ago, a fire destroyed most of a large forest. The animals had no homes. Forest rangers found many young animals, including a small bear who was clinging to a half-burned tree. He was quite scared! They **rescued** the little cub and decided to name him Smokey.

Today Smokey is famous. You may see his picture on posters and T.V. ads. He reminds us to prevent forest fires.

1. **The best title for this story is:**
   a. Smokey the Bear
   b. Forest Fires
   c. Preventing Forest Fires
   d. Life in the Forest

2. **The little bear was found:**
   a. during the fire
   b. clinging to a tree
   c. by a small child
   d. by the roadside

3. **While the forest was burning the little animal was:**
   a. happy
   b. tired
   c. frightened
   d. mad

4. **Smokey is famous because:**
   a. he fights fires
   b. he protects the forest
   c. his picture reminds us to prevent fires
   d. he is a cute bear

5. **In the story, the word "rescued" means:**
   a. ran away
   b. saved
   c. held
   d. found

6. **If this particular bear cub had not been found:**
   a. people would not prevent forest fires
   b. we would use a deer instead of Smokey
   c. we would not use Smokey
   d. both A and B

Page 36

# Answer Key

Name _____

Making potato prints is a lot of fun. First you cut a potato in half. Draw a design on one of the **flat** halves. Cut away the potato around the design. A small knife would be the best tool. Put poster paint on the design with a brush. Print it on paper.

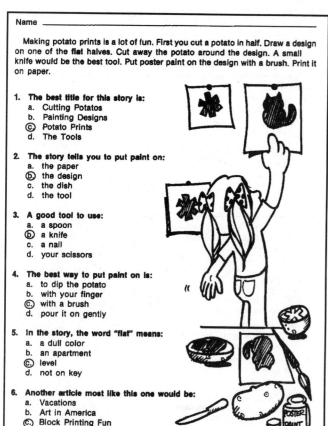

1. **The best title for this story is:**
   a. Cutting Potatos
   b. Painting Designs
   c. Potato Prints
   d. The Tools

2. **The story tells you to put paint on:**
   a. the paper
   b. the design
   c. the dish
   d. the tool

3. **A good tool to use:**
   a. a spoon
   b. a knife
   c. a nail
   d. your scissors

4. **The best way to put paint on is:**
   a. to dip the potato
   b. with your finger
   c. with a brush
   d. pour it on gently

5. **In the story, the word "flat" means:**
   a. a dull color
   b. an apartment
   c. level
   d. not on key

6. **Another article most like this one would be:**
   a. Vacations
   b. Art in America
   c. Block Printing Fun
   d. Potato Pancakes

Page 37

---

Name _____

One day Fluffy ran across the **yard**. She saw some birds flying from branch to branch in the old maple tree. Without thinking, Fluffy climbed the tree. The birds flew away. Fluffy tried to get down but she didn't know how. Mrs. Jones tried to help, but she couldn't reach her cat. She decided to call the Fire Department for help.

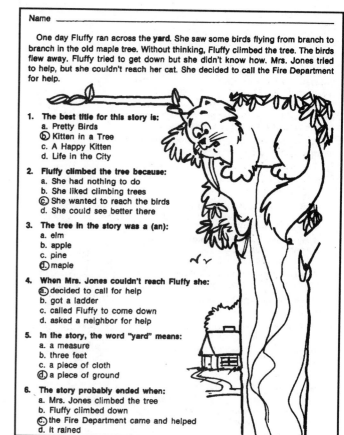

1. **The best title for this story is:**
   a. Pretty Birds
   b. Kitten in a Tree
   c. A Happy Kitten
   d. Life in the City

2. **Fluffy climbed the tree because:**
   a. She had nothing to do
   b. She liked climbing trees
   c. She wanted to reach the birds
   d. She could see better there

3. **The tree in the story was a (an):**
   a. elm
   b. apple
   c. pine
   d. maple

4. **When Mrs. Jones couldn't reach Fluffy she:**
   a. decided to call for help
   b. got a ladder
   c. called Fluffy to come down
   d. asked a neighbor for help

5. **In the story, the word "yard" means:**
   a. a measure
   b. three feet
   c. a piece of cloth
   d. a piece of ground

6. **The story probably ended when:**
   a. Mrs. Jones climbed the tree
   b. Fluffy climbed down
   c. the Fire Department came and helped
   d. it rained

Page 38

---

Name _____

In the **fall**, leaves drop to the ground. Animals may begin to store food. Days become shorter. Cold weather is coming and many birds fly south. People wear warmer clothing and prepare for winter. In some areas there may be rain or even snow, but in many southern areas it is still warm.

1. **The best title for the story is:**
   a. Winter
   b. Birds Fly South
   c. Fall
   d. Animal Habits

2. **Before winter comes, birds may:**
   a. fly north
   b. fly south
   c. store nuts
   d. wear warm clothing

3. **Birds go to places:**
   a. with shorter days
   b. with warmer climate
   c. with more trees
   d. with more snow

4. **People prepare by:**
   a. flying south
   b. wearing warmer clothes
   c. storing food
   d. feeding birds

5. **In the story, the word "fall" means:**
   a. drop to the ground
   b. trip
   c. cold
   d. a season

6. **Animals probably know when winter is coming because:**
   a. the calendar tells them
   b. the leaves fall
   c. they seem to sense a change
   d. it snows

Page 39

---

Name _____

"All that running around has made me hungry," Jimmy told Danny. "Let's make ourselves some lunch. We'll make a sandwich with everything we like best on it. Here is the bread. Now get some peanut butter and jelly. What next?"

Jimmy found a banana and put that on the bread. Then Danny got two chocolate cookies and one Mr. Twinkle cupcake and pressed them down on the banana, and to top it off, he added Captain Quack Potato Chips.

"My mouth is watering! Let's eat." Danny lifted up the sandwich. Splat! The bottom piece of bread had a hole in it. "Next time, we'll just make a ham and cheese sandwich so we won't have to clean up this mess," sighed Danny.

1. **The best name for this story would be:**
   a. Making Chocolate Chip Cookies
   b. Eating Lunch at Home
   c. A Super Sandwich

2. **Jimmy put a lot of _sweets_ on his sandwich.**
   a. sweets
   b. straws
   c. meat

3. **What did Jimmy put on the very top?**
   a. potato chips
   b. chocolate cookies
   c. a banana

4. **"My mouth is watering!" What does this mean?**
   a. Danny is very hungry.
   b. Danny wants something to drink.
   c. Danny hurt his tooth.

5. **The story does not say, but you can tell that:**
   a. The sandwich was too heavy for the bread.
   b. Jimmy went out for lunch every day.
   c. The boys forgot to put on catsup.

Page 40

---

**114**

# Answer Key

Dogs have been "man's best friend" for thousands of years. They have earned man's love and respect because of their faithfulness and devotion. Many dogs have given their lives to save their masters.

Dogs **guard** the home, cattle and sheep. Their keen sense of smell makes them good for hunting animals. They like to be with people and often greet us with barks and wagging tails.

Dogs were the first animals to be tamed by man and are fifth in intelligence among animals.

1. **The best title for this story is:**
   a. Hunting Dogs
   b. Pets
   c. Intelligent Animals
   d. Dogs ✓

2. **Dogs are ___fifth___ in intelligence among animals:**
   a. first
   b. third
   c. fifth ✓
   d. fourth

3. **They are good to take along on hunting trips because:**
   a. they like people
   b. they have a good sense of smell ✓
   c. they like animals
   d. they enjoy trips

4. **They have earned man's love and respect because:**
   a. they are faithful and devoted ✓
   b. we like them
   c. they were the first tame animals
   d. they have been here a long time

5. **In the story, the word "guard" means:**
   a. a man who protects things
   b. a soldier
   c. to watch over ✓
   d. protect with a gun

6. **We can guess a dog enjoys company:**
   a. by his barks
   b. by his intelligence
   c. by his wagging tail
   d. by two of these answers ✓

Page 41

---

Last summer we took a **trip** to Hawaii. We boarded a jet and traveled for many hours.

In Hawaii we saw many new things. We saw a rain forest and an active volcano. We played in the sand and swam in the very warm water.

We took many photographs so we could remember our trip forever. We had to come home all too soon.

1. **The best title for this story is:**
   a. Hawaii's Climate
   b. Flying in a Jet
   c. Our Trip to Hawaii ✓
   d. Visiting a Rain Forest

2. **The first thing the story writer did in the story was:**
   a. board the jet ✓
   b. pack his clothes
   c. buy plane tickets
   d. plan the trip

3. **He can always remember the trip because:**
   a. they were there a long time
   b. they took many photographs ✓
   c. it was their first trip
   d. Hawaii is a nice place to visit

4. **Because of the weather, a good item of clothing to have along would have been:**
   a. a hat ✓
   b. item of clothing
   c. a heavy coat
   d. a ski suit

5. **In the story, the word "trip" means:**
   a. stumble
   b. fall down
   c. set off
   d. a journey ✓

6. **From the story it sounds like the writer:**
   a. is a photographer
   b. was frightened by the volcano
   c. was sorry the trip had to end ✓
   d. takes many trips

Page 42

---

In almost every part of the world, children play with dolls. They may be made of anything from cookie dough to plastic, wood, or rubber. They may be made at home or purchased in the stores that bought the dolls from factories.

Children like to play "grownup" with their dolls. They sew for them, sing to them and even pretend the dolls can talk. Dolls are a **comfort** to the sick and amuse the well. They belong to the rich and poor alike.

1. **The best title for this story is:**
   a. Dolls of Yesterday
   b. Dolls ✓
   c. Playthings
   d. Making Dolls

2. **The story says children use dolls to:**
   a. pretend to be grown-ups ✓
   b. as a substitute for friends
   c. learn sewing
   d. be grown up

3. **After reading the article, we learn that dolls are most preferred by:**
   a. boys
   b. rich children
   c. poor children
   d. rich and poor alike ✓

4. **Dolls are made from:**
   a. mostly wood
   b. many things ✓
   c. mostly dough
   d. mostly plastic

5. **In the story, the word "comfort" means:**
   a. medicine
   b. a blanket
   c. relief from sadness ✓
   d. happy

6. **After reading the article, we can assume:**
   a. the best dolls are made of plastic
   b. dolls may be like friends ✓
   c. you should make your own dolls
   d. dolls were invented in America

Page 43

---

Flying fish do not actually fly as birds do. The fish throws itself from the water with the motion of its strong tail. Once it is in the air it spreads large fins, which act like the wings of a glider. This glide through the air may take the fish 150 to 1,000 feet.

Flying fish live in warm seas. They generally swim in **schools**. The California flying fish grows to be about 18 inches long. Flying fish make excellent food. Many visitors to Catalina Island take a special trip to view flying fish after dark. Huge searchlights are flashed on the ocean so the fish are easy to see.

1. **A good title for this article is:**
   a. A Fish that Really Flies
   b. Flying Fish ✓
   c. Fishing in California
   d. Warm Water Fish

2. **The flying fish doesn't actually:**
   a. swim
   b. glide
   c. fly ✓
   d. sail

3. **The flying fish trip described above is made in:**
   a. the morning
   b. the afternoon
   c. the evening or at night ✓
   d. any time of day

4. **Flying fish have large fins that help them:**
   a. fly
   b. swim
   c. glide through the air
   d. probably both B and C ✓

5. **In the article, the word "schools" means:**
   a. places to learn
   b. groups ✓
   c. large buildings
   d. areas

6. **The fish may glide as many as:**
   a. a hundred feet
   b. a hundred and fifty feet
   c. a thousand feet ✓
   d. two hundred feet

Page 44

---

**115**

# Answer Key

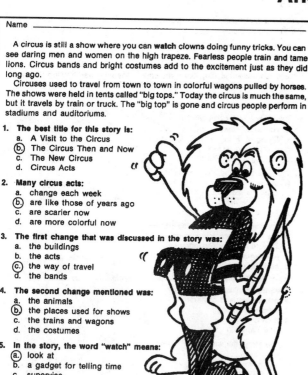
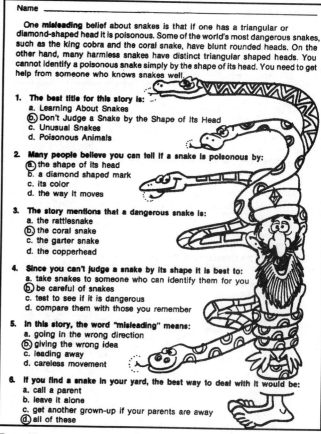

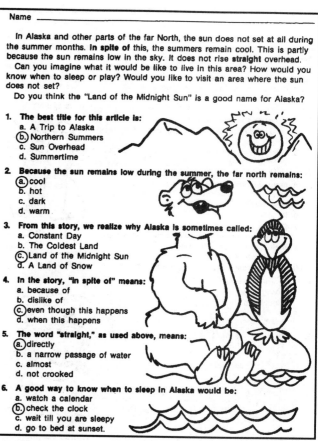

# Answer Key

## Page 49

**Name** _____

"We missed you at school last Tuesday, Chip," Mrs. Decker said. "How did you break your arm, falling out of a tree? Sit down and tell me what happened to you."

"Two nights ago, when it was very late and I was sound asleep, an alligator came through my window. He was just about to take a big bite out of my toe when I spotted him at the bottom of my bed. So I jumped up and started to bark like a dog. That alligator sure hurried to get out the window again, but I forgot to move out of his way and he knocked me over with his tail. When I opened my eyes, there I was lying on the floor. From now on, I'm going to lock my window at night!"

1. **A good name for this story would be:**
   a. Chip Breaks His Arm *(circled)*
   b. An Alligator Eats Chip
   c. Barking Scares Alligators

2. **Chip tried to** _scare_ **the alligator.**
   a. bite
   b. scare *(circled)*
   c. make friends with

3. **When did the alligator come through the window?**
   a. in the afternoon
   b. on Monday
   c. very late *(circled)*

4. **Tail means "something that wags." Tale means:**
   a. a story *(circled)*
   b. a test
   c. a book

5. **The story does not say, but you can guess that**
   a. Chip was having a nightmare. *(circled)*
   b. Chip lived in the jungle.
   c. Chip did not really have a broken arm.

YIKES!

**Page 49**

## Page 50

**Name** _____

Mr. Anderson bought a camera for his son Scott. Scott went down the street and started shooting pictures. Suddenly, he heard someone scream.

"Stop that thief; he has my dog," yelled a woman.

Scott saw a man dashing down the street. The man was holding a silver poodle. Scott put his foot in the man's **path** as he ran past. The man dropped the dog.

The man jumped up and ran away, but Scott got a picture of him before he disappeared. The woman thanked Scott for his help.

1. **The most interesting title for this story is:**
   a. Scott and His Camera
   b. Scott Gets a Present
   c. The Boy Who Saved a Dog *(circled)*
   d. A Happy Day

2. **Scott was on the street when a dog was stolen because:**
   a. he liked to play outside
   b. his father told him to go
   c. he heard someone scream
   d. he was trying his new camera *(circled)*

3. **When Scott tripped the man and later took his picture, it proved:**
   a. he could think quickly *(circled)*
   b. he was good with a camera
   c. he liked dogs
   d. he always helped others

4. **The lady thanked Scott because:**
   a. he was a friend of hers
   b. he saved her dog *(circled)*
   c. the picture helped catch the thief
   d. he took her picture

5. **In this story, the word "path" means:**
   a. a walkway
   b. a direction of traveling *(circled)*
   c. a road made by traveling an area often
   d. a way of life

6. **Even though what Scott did turned out well:**
   a. it was perfectly safe
   b. it could have been dangerous *(circled)*
   c. it would be good to try
   d. it would be good for everyone to do

**Page 50**

## Page 51

**Name** _____

Grizzly bears are massive animals native to western North America. Large numbers of these great beasts once roamed the western states, but only a few hundred remain in the United States today.

Grizzly bears may grow up to 8 feet tall and weigh 800 pounds. These bears are, of course, very frightening. Their coat varies from creamy brown to almost black. Their **limbs** are dark. Their fur is often tipped with white and thus they are sometimes called silver-tips.

Although few of these bears remain in the United States, more of them live in Alaska and Canada.

1. **The most interesting title for this story would be:**
   a. Grizzly Bears
   b. The Disappearing Grizzly *(circled)*
   c. Bears of North America
   d. In the Woods

2. **A very frightening thing about a grizzly can be his:**
   a. cry
   b. size *(circled)*
   c. fur
   d. color

3. **The bears are sometimes called silver tips because:**
   a. their fur is tipped with silver
   b. they live in a land of silver
   c. they have a touch of white on their fur that may look like silver *(circled)*
   d. their ears have silver tips

4. **There are now:**
   a. more grizzlies in North America
   b. less grizzlies in the United States *(circled)*
   c. more bears in Mexico
   d. fewer bears in Alaska

5. **In the story, the word "limbs" means:**
   a. parts of a tree
   b. arms
   c. legs
   d. parts similar to arms and legs *(circled)*

6. **We can assume that a grizzly would be:**
   a. very dangerous *(circled)*
   b. very popular
   c. found mainly in South America
   d. friendly

**Page 51**

## Page 52

**Name** _____

As we were driving along the **deserted** country road, we saw a spooky house. There seemed to be a face peering at us from a window. We began to shake with fear. Suddenly our car stopped. We had run out of gas. There seemed to be no place to go, so with our teeth chattering, we approached the scary house. The door was open. We went in.

Something bumped into me and I spun around. I realized that it was only an old cow that had been trapped inside accidentally.

1. **The best title for this story is:**
   a. A Trip to the Country
   b. A Spooky Adventure *(circled)*
   c. Faces in the Night
   d. Chattering Teeth

2. **The face peered from the:**
   a. door
   b. barn
   c. window *(circled)*
   d. basement

3. **The writer's teeth were chattering because:**
   a. he was cold
   b. he was scared *(circled)*
   c. he was trying to make noise
   d. he had a toothache

4. **The cow:**
   a. couldn't find a way out *(circled)*
   b. lived in the house
   c. liked warm places
   d. came in to scare someone

5. **In the story, the word "deserted" means:**
   a. a dry land
   b. a sweet food
   c. abandoned *(circled)*
   d. scary

6. **The writer probably entered the spooky house:**
   a. to phone for or get help *(circled)*
   b. because he likes scary places
   c. for fun
   d. because he wanted to rest

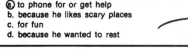

**Page 52**

**117**

FS-32044 Reading

# Answer Key

Name

Scientists have **advanced** many reasons to explain why dinosaurs died out. The main cause was probably the rise of mountain ranges during the Cretaceous period. When mountains formed, great seaways drained the vast swamplands and they dried up. This caused many changes in climate and food supply. The dinosaurs could not adjust. The plant eaters could not eat the new plants so many died. Then those that ate the plant eaters did not have enough food. This long slow process took about 10 to 20 million years.

1. **The best title for this story is:**
   a. What Dinosaurs Ate
   b. Living Long Ago
   c. Why Dinosaurs Died Off
   d. How Mountains Formed
2. **Many dinosaurs didn't have food because:**
   a. other animals ate it
   b. the swamplands dried up
   c. the seas became larger
   d. all the food was soured
3. **Meat eating dinosaurs died because:**
   a. the plant eaters died
   b. they ate plants
   c. the animals were in the hills
   d. they ate too much
4. **This long process took about:**
   a. 5 million years
   b. 1 to 2 million years
   c. 25 million years
   d. 10 to 20 million years
5. **In the story, the word "advanced" means:**
   a. walked forward
   b. suggested or proposed
   c. moved ahead in space
   d. know for sure
6. **The information man has written about dinosaurs is:**
   a. all true
   b. just a story for children
   c. assumed from things people have found
   d. mostly false

Page 53

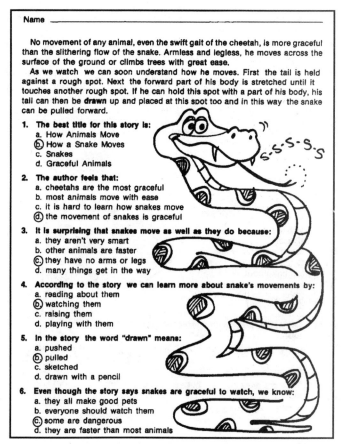

Name

No movement of any animal, even the swift gait of the cheetah, is more graceful than the slithering flow of the snake. Armless and legless, he moves across the surface of the ground or climbs trees with great ease.

As we watch we can soon understand how he moves. First the tail is held against a rough spot. Next the forward part of his body is stretched until it touches another rough spot. If he can hold this spot with a part of his body, his tail can then be **drawn** up and placed at this spot too and in this way the snake can be pulled forward.

1. **The best title for this story is:**
   a. How Animals Move
   b. How a Snake Moves
   c. Snakes
   d. Graceful Animals
2. **The author feels that:**
   a. cheetahs are the most graceful
   b. most animals move with ease
   c. it is hard to learn how snakes move
   d. the movement of snakes is graceful
3. **It is surprising that snakes move as well as they do because:**
   a. they aren't very smart
   b. other animals are faster
   c. they have no arms or legs
   d. many things get in the way
4. **According to the story we can learn more about snake's movements by:**
   a. reading about them
   b. watching them
   c. raising them
   d. playing with them
5. **In the story the word "drawn" means:**
   a. pushed
   b. pulled
   c. sketched
   d. drawn with a pencil
6. **Even though the story says snakes are graceful to watch, we know:**
   a. they all make good pets
   b. everyone should watch them
   c. some are dangerous
   d. they are faster than most animals

Page 54

Name

The metric system is a group of units used to make any kind of measurement. It is said to be one of the simplest of measurements ever used. The metric system is used in all major countries with the exception of the United States.

The metric system was created by French scientists in the 1790's. The word metric comes from the basic unit of length in the system, the meter.

The metric system may **seem** difficult if you have not used it. This is because you are not familiar with the units. Once you use the system, it becomes easier to understand.

1. **The best title for this story is:**
   a. The Metric System
   b. New Ways to Measure
   c. Understanding Measurement
   d. The French Measurement
2. **The author suggests that:**
   a. it is hard to use this system
   b. the United States should learn the system
   c. it is easier to use the system after you are familiar with it
   d. it would probably be too hard to learn
3. **The system is popular because:**
   a. it was begun by Americans
   b. it was begun by the French
   c. it can be used for any kind of measurement
   d. everyone understands it
4. **The system originally began in:**
   a. The United States
   b. France
   c. in all countries except the U.S.
   d. England
5. **The word "seem" means:**
   a. appear to be
   b. a line of sewing
   c. is really
   d. none of these
6. **Since so many countries use the metric system, it is possible:**
   a. the U.S. may some day use it
   b. the U.S. will never use it
   c. the U.S. must use it to be popular
   d. other countries will change to our system

Page 55

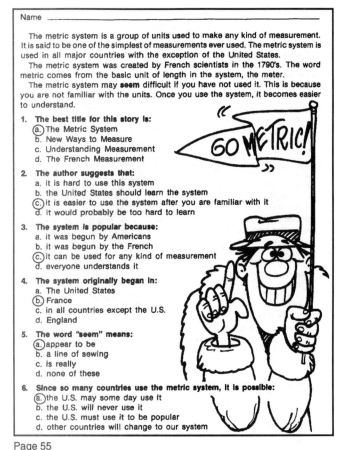

GO METRIC!

Name _____ Date _____

### A Friendly Snake

One day, I was lying under a tree. Suddenly, I felt something lick my face. I opened one eye. (Gasp! Gulp!) It was a snake. A huge green snake! He just sat there looking at me. His tongue was hanging out. Did he want to play? "Hello," I said in a brave voice. "My name is Danny." The snake slurped his tongue back in his mouth. "Hi, there," he answered. "I'm Ralph."

I was just about to scream. Then I woke up.

1. **What is the main idea of this story?**
   a. a snake that talks
   b. sleeping under a tree
   c. a funny dream
2. **Another word for <u>scream</u> is:**
   a. yell
   b. search
   c. sing
3. **Danny was very surprised because:**
   a. The snake talked.
   b. The snake was green.
   c. The snake screamed.
4. **Where was Danny lying?**

   Danny was lying under a tree.

5. **What did Ralph look like?**

   Ralph was huge and green.

6. **Find three sounds in the story.**

   Gasp! Gulp! Slurped!

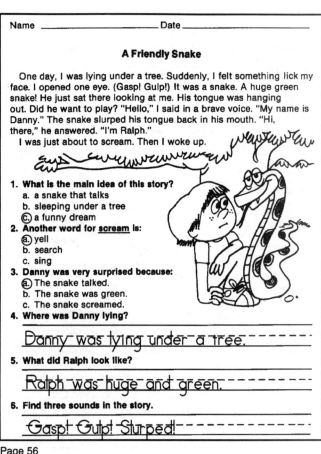

Page 56

# Answer Key

### A Spider's Adventure

"I want to go to the park. How am I going to cross the street?" wondered the spider. "The cars are going too fast." Just then, a shoe appeared. "Perfect! I'll pop on this shoe." Thump. Squish. Thump. Squish. The shoe started running. It went faster and faster. "Help! Let me off!" screamed the spider, but the shoe ran on and on. One hour later, it finally stopped. "I'll never take a shoe anywhere again!" sputtered the spider. "Next time, I'm taking the bus."

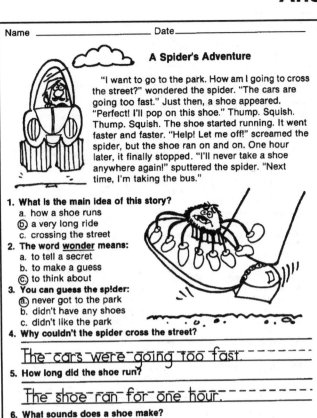

1. **What is the main idea of this story?**
   a. how a shoe runs
   b. a very long ride
   c. crossing the street
2. **The word wonder means:**
   a. to tell a secret
   b. to make a guess
   c. to think about
3. **You can guess the spider:**
   a. never got to the park
   b. didn't have any shoes
   c. didn't like the park
4. **Why couldn't the spider cross the street?**

The cars were going too fast.

5. **How long did the shoe run?**

The shoe ran for one hour.

6. **What sounds does a shoe make?**

thump and squish

Page 57

---

### Little Lost Egg

One bright sunny day, a goose went out walking. She saw something under a tree. "A little lost egg!" she cried. "I'll sit on it and keep it warm." After three days, the egg cracked open. Out jumped a kangaroo. "I'll find your mother," said the goose. Away she flew. When the goose looked down, the kangaroo was gone. The goose turned around. There was the kangaroo, right behind her. He was flying! "He thinks I'm his mother. I might as well keep him. I can teach him to say 'Honk! honk!' like me."

1. **What is the main idea of this story?**
   a. a new mother
   b. a walking goose
   c. a flying kangaroo
2. **The opposite of lost is:**
   a. found
   b. lose
   c. forgot
3. **The kangaroo will learn how to:**
   a. look like a goose
   b. walk like a goose
   c. sound like a goose
4. **Where was the egg?**

The egg was under a tree.

5. **What kind of day is it in the story?**

It is a bright sunny day.

6. **How long did the goose sit on the egg?**

The goose sat on the egg for three days.

Page 58

---

### Ping-Pong, Anyone?

Ho-hum. Another day on this dusty old shelf. Doesn't anyone need a size 13 AAAA green shoe? Wait a minute. I hear a voice. "Do you have a good shoe for playing football?" a tall man asked. Uh-oh. I don't like football. I'll get stomped on! Tramped on! "Nice shoe," said the man. "But it doesn't go with my clothes." Phew! Saved! I'd make a good ping-pong shoe. I won't get hurt playing ping-pong.

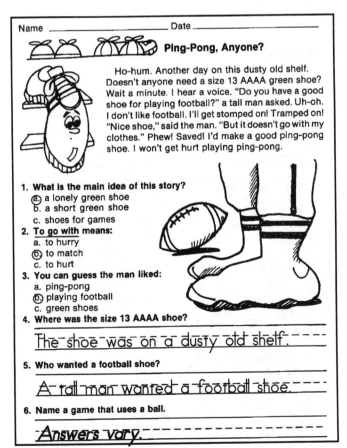

1. **What is the main idea of this story?**
   a. a lonely green shoe
   b. a short green shoe
   c. shoes for games
2. **To go with means:**
   a. to hurry
   b. to match
   c. to hurt
3. **You can guess the man liked:**
   a. ping-pong
   b. playing football
   c. green shoes
4. **Where was the size 13 AAAA shoe?**

The shoe was on a dusty old shelf.

5. **Who wanted a football shoe?**

A tall man wanted a football shoe.

6. **Name a game that uses a ball.**

Answers vary.

Page 59

---

### Summer Fun!

Dear Mom and Dad,
   Here I am at camp. It was a long trip yesterday. First, the bus driver got lost. He went to the wrong camp. It was for boys. Finally, we got to our camp. It was late at night. I found 300 frogs sitting in my tent. They wouldn't leave. So I left. This morning, guess what happened? My sleeping bag wouldn't unzip. I could be stuck in here forever! Camp is fun. Wish you were here.

Love,
Nancy

1. **What is the main idea of this story?**
   a. a letter to Nancy
   b. riding on a bus
   c. a letter from camp
2. **To wish means to:**
   a. have
   b. want
   c. give
3. **Nancy has been at camp:**
   a. for two days
   b. for one night
   c. a long time
4. **What was in Nancy's tent?**

There were 300 frogs in Nancy's tent.

5. **Who got lost?**

The bus driver got lost.

6. **When did Nancy get to camp?**

Nancy got to camp late at night.

Page 60

# Answer Key

---

Name _____ Date _____

### Great Day for Moving

"Everybody up!" called Thurmond, the chief
turtle. "This is moving day. Ozzie, you take
the pillows. Della can pack the suitcases. The chairs
and lamps will be Wally's. I'll take the piano.
We'd better get going. Our new home is three blocks
away. It will take us one month to get there.
I hope it doesn't snow. Then it will take us
two months."

1. **What is the main idea of this story?**
   a. packing up chairs
   b. getting ready to move ✓
   c. moving in a month
2. **To pack means the same as:**
   a. fill up ✓
   b. set out
   c. move around
3. **You can guess the turtles:**
   a. like the snow
   b. move once a year
   c. move very slowly ✓
4. **What did Wally carry?**

   _Wally carried the chairs and lamps._

5. **How far are the turtles moving?**

   _They are moving three blocks away._

6. **Thurmond hopes it won't snow. Why?**

   _It will take two months to move._

Page 61

---

Name _____ Date _____

### Brusha Brusha

Terri Jean works at a zoo. She has a special job. Every Monday, Terri
walks into the hippo pond. "OK, Higby. Open your mouth," says
Terri. "Wider! Wider! Now I can brush your teeth for you." Terri pulls out
a giant toothbrush. She squeezes Plum Patootie toothpaste on it.
That is Higby's favorite. It is very sweet. For ten minutes Terri rubs and
scrubs. "All clean, Higby. Let me see you smile. How beautiful!
Your teeth really sparkle."

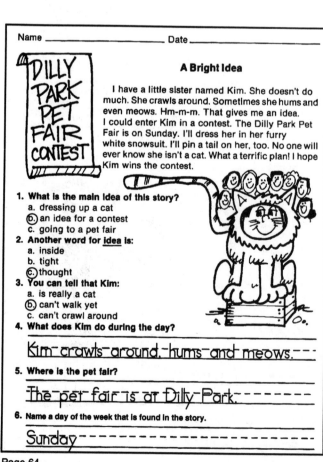

1. **What is the main idea of this story?**
   a. cleaning the hippo pond
   b. cleaning Higby's teeth ✓
   c. a job at the zoo
2. **The word sparkle can also mean:**
   a. to brush
   b. to clean
   c. to shine ✓
3. **Higby would probably like the taste of:**
   a. lemon
   b. pepper
   c. honey ✓
4. **Where does Terri work?**

   _Terri works at the zoo._

5. **What is Terri's job?**

   _Terri's job is brushing Higby's teeth._

6. **Name a day of the week found in the story.**

   _Monday_

Page 62

---

Name _____ Date _____

### What's for Breakfast?

Every morning, my mother makes breakfast for me. She fixes breakfast
for the cat, the dog and the bird, too. Yesterday, Mother was in a big
rush. She cooked everything very fast. "Barbie, breakfast is ready!" she
called. There was a dog dish at my place on the table. The bird had a
dish of milk. The cat had birdseed. The dog had eggs. They ate
up everything! I don't like dog food. I guess I'll have some cake. (I'm glad
the dog ate my eggs.)

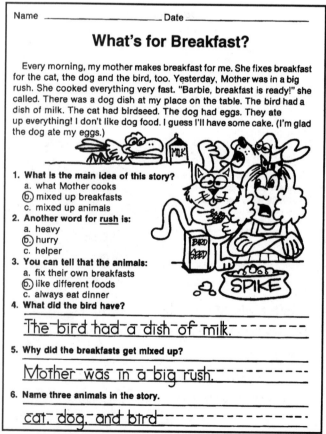

1. **What is the main idea of this story?**
   a. what Mother cooks
   b. mixed up breakfasts ✓
   c. mixed up animals
2. **Another word for rush is:**
   a. heavy
   b. hurry ✓
   c. helper
3. **You can tell that the animals:**
   a. fix their own breakfasts
   b. like different foods ✓
   c. always eat dinner
4. **What did the bird have?**

   _The bird had a dish of milk._

5. **Why did the breakfasts get mixed up?**

   _Mother was in a big rush._

6. **Name three animals in the story.**

   _cat, dog, and bird_

Page 63

---

Name _____ Date _____

### A Bright Idea

I have a little sister named Kim. She doesn't do
much. She crawls around. Sometimes she hums and
even meows. Hm-m-m. That gives me an idea.
I could enter Kim in a contest. The Dilly Park Pet
Fair is on Sunday. I'll dress her in her furry
white snowsuit. I'll pin a tail on her, too. No one will
ever know she isn't a cat. What a terrific plan! I hope
Kim wins the contest.

1. **What is the main idea of this story?**
   a. dressing up a cat
   b. an idea for a contest ✓
   c. going to a pet fair
2. **Another word for idea is:**
   a. inside
   b. tight
   c. thought ✓
3. **You can tell that Kim:**
   a. is really a cat
   b. can't walk yet ✓
   c. can't crawl around
4. **What does Kim do during the day?**

   _Kim crawls around, hums and meows._

5. **Where is the pet fair?**

   _The pet fair is at Dilly Park._

6. **Name a day of the week that is found in the story.**

   _Sunday_

Page 64

---

**120**

# Answer Key

## Feeling Better?

My mom went out tonight just before dark. I am babysitting my sister Judy. Judy is sick. "Will pizza make you feel better?" I asked. After two bites, Judy felt terrible. Next I fixed some gumdrop cookies. These made her really sick! Let's see . . . I have one more idea— a peanut butter and banana sandwich. That will make her all better. What a good brother I am!

1. **What is the main idea of this story?**
   a. a sick mother
   (b) a thoughtful brother
   c. a pizza for dinner
2. **Another word for** <u>idea</u> **is:**
   (a) plan
   b. work
   c. sick
3. **From the story you can tell:**
   a. Mother went out late.
   b. Cookies will make you well.
   (c) Food made Judy sicker.
4. **What kind of sandwich did the boy make?**

The boy made a peanut butter and banana sandwich.

5. **When did Mother leave?**

Mother left just before dark.

6. **What made Judy really sick?**

Gumdrop cookies made Judy really sick.

Page 65

## Tall Tales

What is a tall tale? Many tall tales are wild stories that people just make up. They may be about a huge fish they almost caught. Tall tales are often about people who really lived long ago. Over the years, the adventures that they had just seemed to get bigger and bigger. After awhile, no one knew what was true and what wasn't. Sometimes tall tales are about people who never lived. No one knows how some of these stories got started. Tall tales are fun. Many of the stories you think just can't be true. They make us laugh. They make us wonder. Did Johnny Appleseed really plant so many trees? Did Paul Bunyan really have a blue ox? Was John Henry that strong? Every country has tall tales. The ones you will learn about in this book took place in North America.

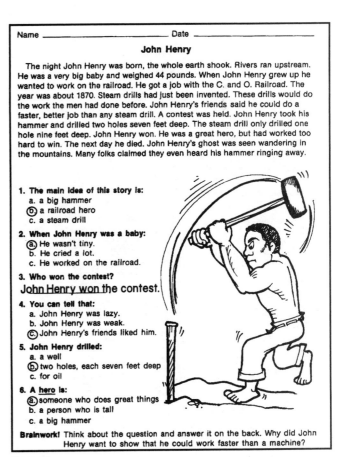

1. **The main idea of this story is:**
   a. about Johnny and his seeds
   (b) about tall tales
   c. about many countries
2. **Many tall tales are:**
   (a) hard to believe
   b. about you and me
   c. sad
3. **John Henry was supposed to be**
   strong.
4. **You can guess that:**
   a. There are not many tall tales.
   (b) Tall tales are often very old.
   c. Tall tales are always about animals.
5. **Paul Bunyan had a:**
   a. blue goat
   b. yellow bird
   (c) blue ox
6. **An** <u>ox</u> **is:**
   (a) a kind of bull
   b. an apple
   c. a small person

**Brainwork!** Think about the question. Answer it on the back. Write a tall tale about a fish that got away.

Page 66

## Johnny Appleseed

John Chapman knew everything about trees. Fruit trees were his favorite kinds of trees. Each day he saw people heading west as they passed his Pennsylvania farm. John felt sorry for these pioneers. He knew they'd see hard times. He started giving away apple seeds. This way, people could plant beautiful orchards wherever they'd go. Soon, John gave up his farm and roamed all over the country. He planted seeds and gave people the baby trees. No one called him John Chapman anymore. His name had become Johnny Appleseed forever. Johnny was a strange sight. He slept out in the open in all weather. He wore no shoes. He carried his cooking pot by wearing it on his head. Johnny had a pet wolf, too. One day Johnny died while he was tending his trees. Some folks say they still see his ghost walking through the apple orchards of Indiana and Ohio.

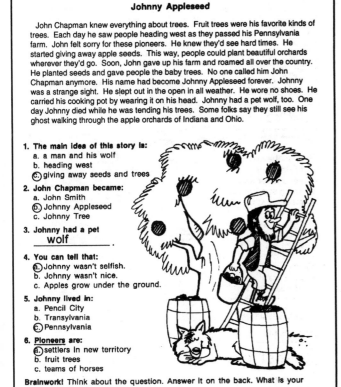

1. **The main idea of this story is:**
   a. a man and his wolf
   b. heading west
   (c) giving away seeds and trees
2. **John Chapman became:**
   a. John Smith
   (b) Johnny Appleseed
   c. Johnny Tree
3. **Johnny had a pet**
   wolf.
4. **You can tell that:**
   (a) Johnny wasn't selfish.
   b. Johnny wasn't nice.
   c. Apples grow under the ground.
5. **Johnny lived in:**
   a. Pencil City
   b. Transylvania
   (c) Pennsylvania
6. **Pioneers are:**
   (a) settlers in new territory
   b. fruit trees
   c. teams of horses

**Brainwork!** Think about the question. Answer it on the back. What is your favorite tree? Why?

Page 67

## John Henry

The night John Henry was born, the whole earth shook. Rivers ran upstream. He was a very big baby and weighed 44 pounds. When John Henry grew up he wanted to work on the railroad. He got a job with the C. and O. Railroad. The year was about 1870. Steam drills had just been invented. These drills would do the work the men had done before. John Henry's friends said he could do a faster, better job than any steam drill. A contest was held. John Henry took his hammer and drilled two holes seven feet deep. The steam drill only drilled one hole nine feet deep. John Henry won. He was a great hero, but had worked too hard to win. The next day he died. John Henry's ghost was seen wandering in the mountains. Many folks claimed they even heard his hammer ringing away.

1. **The main idea of this story is:**
   a. a big hammer
   (b) a railroad hero
   c. a steam drill
2. **When John Henry was a baby:**
   (a) He wasn't tiny.
   b. He cried a lot.
   c. He worked on the railroad.
3. **Who won the contest?**
   John Henry won the contest.
4. **You can tell that:**
   a. John Henry was lazy.
   b. John Henry was weak.
   (c) John Henry's friends liked him.
5. **John Henry drilled:**
   a. a well
   (b) two holes, each seven feet deep
   c. for oil
6. **A** <u>hero</u> **is:**
   (a) someone who does great things
   b. a person who is tall
   c. a big hammer

**Brainwork!** Think about the question and answer it on the back. Why did John Henry want to show that he could work faster than a machine?

Page 68

# Answer Key

**122**

---

Name _____ Date _____

## Rip Van Winkle

If you think you like to sleep a lot, just listen to this story. "Rip Van Winkle" is an old tale from the Catskill mountains of New York. One day, Rip walked to the woods to get away from his wife. She scolded him all the time. Rip saw strange little men in the woods. They offered him a drink. He fell asleep. When he woke up, he felt stiff. Rip walked back to his village, but the place had changed. He saw no one he knew. Finally, Rip found out the truth. He had taken a nap for twenty years! Rip found his daughter. She was so happy to see her father. Rip's wife had been dead for years. He went to live with his daughter. He told his strange story over and over again for many happy years.

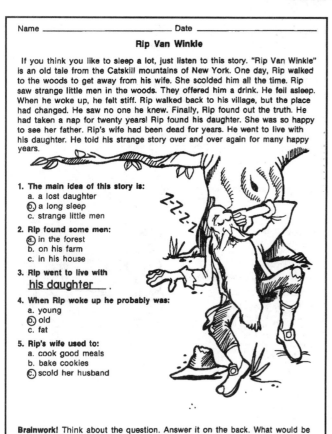

1. The main idea of this story is:
   a. a lost daughter
   ⓑ a long sleep
   c. strange little men

2. Rip found some men:
   ⓐ in the forest
   b. on his farm
   c. in his house

3. Rip went to live with
   **his daughter** .

4. When Rip woke up he probably was:
   a. young
   ⓑ old
   c. fat

5. Rip's wife used to:
   a. cook good meals
   b. bake cookies
   ⓒ scold her husband

**Brainwork!** Think about the question. Answer it on the back. What would be bad about sleeping for twenty years?

Page 69

---

Name _____ Date _____

## Paul Bunyan

This is just one story about the biggest, strongest man anywhere. Paul Bunyan was a lumberjack. He could cut down more trees than anyone. Paul and his giant blue ox, Babe, chopped down trees. They cut them into logs and took them to the sawmills. Paul even changed the map of America. Once, on a walk to Louisiana, Paul got sand in his shoes. He dumped out the sand. That pile of sand grew to be the Kiamichi Mountains of Oklahoma. Babe helped, too. When he walked he made very large footprints. People think that dinosaurs made them, but it was Babe, of course. One day, Babe got very sick. Paul cried. His tears made the Great Salt Lake of Utah! One day Babe knocked over a big tank of water. Paul dug a big ditch for the water. That ditch is known as the Mississippi River! The dirt that came from the ditch made the Rocky Mountains!

1. The main idea of this story is:
   a. a big ox
   ⓑ a great man
   c. a big ditch

2. Paul cried when:
   ⓐ Babe didn't feel well.
   b. He saw dinosaurs.
   c. He got sand in his shoes.

3. Paul Bunyan was a
   **lumberjack** .

4. You can tell that:
   a. Paul was lazy.
   ⓑ Paul kept himself busy.
   c. Babe was a red ox.

5. Babe's footprints looked like:
   a. Paul's footprints
   b. logs
   ⓒ dinosaur footprints

6. A **lumberjack:**
   a. bakes cakes
   b. traps bears
   ⓒ cuts down trees

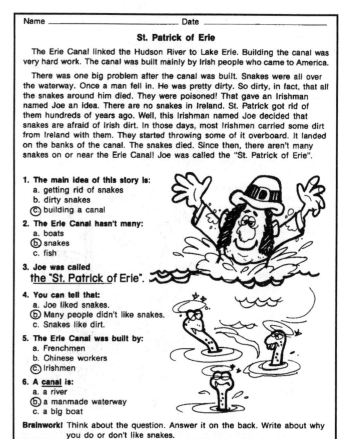

**Brainwork!** Think about the question. Answer it on the back. Write why you think Paul Bunyan could or couldn't have done all those great deeds.

Page 70

---

Name _____ Date _____

## Davy Crockett

Davy was a real person. Tall tales about him were started by Davy himself! Davy once said that he'd killed 105 bears in eight months! By the time Davy died at the Alamo in 1836, he was thought of as a superman!

One day, Davy Crockett said, "Did you ever hear about when I fixed the sun?" His friends shook their heads. They knew this was going to be a good story. "Well," Davy went on, "one day the weather was so cold that everything was frozen solid. The sun was stuck between two pieces of ice. If I didn't get it unstuck fast, everyone would be done for. Well, I took a bear that I'd just killed. I started hitting the ice with it. In about fifteen seconds, the sun got loose. The sun walked up to me and saluted. I put a piece of the sun into my pocket. I carried it along to show everyone the fresh daylight."

1. The main idea of this story is:
   a. a frozen bear
   ⓑ Davy and the sun
   c. a man who was stuck

2. The sun couldn't get out of:
   a. bed
   b. the clouds
   ⓒ some ice

3. Davy said he'd killed
   **105 bears** .

4. You can guess that:
   a. Davy didn't talk much.
   ⓑ Davy liked to brag.
   c. Davy was a bear.

5. Most of the stories were:
   ⓐ started by Davy
   b. told by bears
   c. told by Davy's mother

6. **Saluted** means:
   ⓐ greeted
   b. smiled
   c. stepped on

**Brainwork!** Think about the question. Answer it on the back. Why do you think that Davy's story isn't true?

Page 71

---

Name _____ Date _____

## St. Patrick of Erie

The Erie Canal linked the Hudson River to Lake Erie. Building the canal was very hard work. The canal was built mainly by Irish people who came to America.

There was one big problem after the canal was built. Snakes were all over the waterway. Once a man fell in. He was pretty dirty. So dirty, in fact, that all the snakes around him died. They were poisoned! That gave an Irishman named Joe an idea. There are no snakes in Ireland. St. Patrick got rid of them hundreds of years ago. Well, this Irishman named Joe decided that snakes are afraid of Irish dirt. In those days, most Irishmen carried some dirt from Ireland with them. They started throwing some of it overboard. It landed on the banks of the canal. The snakes died. Since then, there aren't many snakes on or near the Erie Canal! Joe was called the "St. Patrick of Erie".

1. The main idea of this story is:
   a. getting rid of snakes
   b. dirty snakes
   ⓒ building a canal

2. The Erie Canal hasn't many:
   a. boats
   ⓑ snakes
   c. fish

3. Joe was called
   **the "St. Patrick of Erie".**

4. You can tell that:
   a. Joe liked snakes.
   ⓑ Many people didn't like snakes.
   c. Snakes like dirt.

5. The Erie Canal was built by:
   a. Frenchmen
   b. Chinese workers
   ⓒ Irishmen

6. A **canal** is:
   a. a river
   ⓑ a manmade waterway
   c. a big boat

**Brainwork!** Think about the question. Answer it on the back. Write about why you do or don't like snakes.

Page 72

# Answer Key

## Mike Fink

"I love to fight! I'm part wild horse and alligator." Mike Fink, of course, was really a man. He was also the most famous river boatman. Mike bragged a lot about himself. He said, "I can outrun, outshoot, outbrag and outfight any man on the Mississippi River." Mike was always fighting with other boatmen. He even tangled with the great Davy Crockett a few times. One story tells about a shooting contest they had. Each man claimed his gun was best. Davy won that contest. Another time Mike said he could beat Davy in a boat race. Davy beat Mike in that one, too. They ended up as friends. Mike's daughter was just like her father. He sure was proud of her! Writers in the 1800's loved to tell tales about Mike Fink, the most daring of all the boatmen!

1. **The main idea of this story is:**
   a. about Davy Crockett
   b. Mike Fink's daughter
   c. a famous boatman ✓

2. **Mike Fink said he could:**
   a. beat anyone at anything ✓
   b. go around the world
   c. whinny like a horse

3. **Mike Fink was proud of** his daughter .

4. **You can guess that:**
   a. No one liked Mike.
   b. People liked Mike's adventures. ✓
   c. Mike didn't have children.

5. **Mike had contests with:**
   a. Daniel Boone
   b. Paul Bunyan
   c. Davy Crockett ✓

6. **To capture means:**
   a. fight with
   b. catch ✓
   c. set free

**Brainwork!** Think about the question. Answer it on the back. Why do people like to brag about themselves?

Page 73

## Joe Magarac

Joe was the greatest steel man that ever lived. He worked in Pennsylvania. There, most of America's steel is made. Joe was the biggest, toughest steel man. He would stir the boiling hot steel by hand. Then he'd take it and shape it into bars. No one else could do that. Joe ate five meals a day. The rest of the time he'd make steel. Joe made so much steel that his friends got angry. They thought they'd lose their jobs. Joe made all the steel needed. Joe just smiled. "No," he said. "All of America needs steel. We'll just build a bigger mill." But the steel mill was closed. Joe was sad. One day, he jumped into the steel pot. After he melted down, people could hear him laugh. Joe had made the world's strongest steel. A new mill was built. There were enough jobs for everyone. Today, good steel men call each other "magaracs".

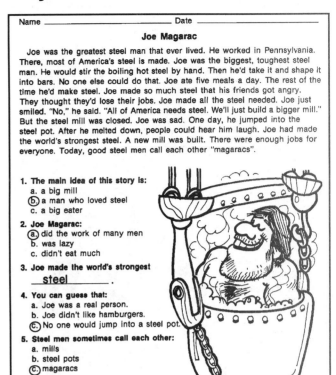

1. **The main idea of this story is:**
   a. a big mill
   b. a man who loved steel ✓
   c. a big eater

2. **Joe Magarac:**
   a. did the work of many men ✓
   b. was lazy
   c. didn't eat much

3. **Joe made the world's strongest** steel .

4. **You can guess that:**
   a. Joe was a real person.
   b. Joe didn't like hamburgers.
   c. No one would jump into a steel pot. ✓

5. **Steel men sometimes call each other:**
   a. mills
   b. steel pots
   c. magaracs ✓

6. **A mill is:**
   a. a place to eat lunch
   b. a building in which steel is made ✓
   c. a kind of steel

**Brainwork!** Think about the question. Answer it on the back. Why did steel workers make up the story about Joe Magarac?

Page 74

## Jean Lafitte the Pirate

Ships that sailed off the coast of Louisiana weren't safe. Their biggest danger was pirate Jean Lafitte. Jean didn't care whose ships he attacked. He did, however, love the United States. Jean told President Jackson he'd help him fight the British. This was during the War of 1812. At first, the president didn't want the help of a pirate! Later, he changed his mind. Jean Lafitte and his men fought bravely. Lafitte became a hero. He had saved New Orleans from the British! After the war, Jean went back to being a pirate. After he died, many people tried to find his treasure of gold and jewels. Once, a soldier said he saw the ghost of Lafitte. The ghost told him where his treasure was. He told him to use it to help people. The soldier ran to town and told everyone. When they raced back to the spot, there was no treasure. They just heard a ghost moaning. The soldier shouldn't have told Jean's secret.

1. **The main idea of this story is:**
   a. buried treasure
   b. the life of a pirate ✓
   c. running from a ghost

2. **Jean Lafitte wanted to:**
   a. help the British
   b. look for a gold mine
   c. help the Americans ✓

3. **The soldier told** Jean's secret .

4. **You can tell that:**
   a. Jean Lafitte was a president.
   b. Jean liked the life of a pirate. ✓
   c. The British liked Jean.

5. **Jean Lafitte attacked:**
   a. airplanes
   b. trains
   c. ships ✓

6. **Moaning is:**
   a. laughing and giggling
   b. yawning out loud
   c. a long, sad sound ✓

**Brainwork!** Think about the question. Answer it on the back. What would you do with Jean Lafitte's treasure if you found it?

Page 75

## Febold Feboldson

Poor Febold really was a nice man. He always tried to help people. His helping never turned out right, though. Once, Febold wanted to get rid of coyotes. He bought some huggags. Now, these animals will take care of all your coyote troubles. They do like to lean on trees, though. There were no trees in Nebraska. Those huggags kept falling down. They were useless against coyotes.

Another time, Febold wanted settlers in Nebraska. He heard people liked gold. He put thousands of goldfish in a river. People riding by thought that gold shine was real gold. They stayed and settled in Nebraska. When they found out what Febold had done, they were mad! Febold did start rain, though. He tricked some frogs into croaking. Everyone knows that brings rain. The people of Nebraska liked Febold for doing that!

1. **The main idea of this story is:**
   a. a bunch of frogs
   b. a strange man ✓
   c. about trees

2. **Febold didn't have:**
   a. any animals
   b. good luck ✓
   c. goldfish

3. **Febold lived in** Nebraska .

4. **You can tell that:**
   a. Febold didn't like people.
   b. People like coyotes.
   c. Febold meant well. ✓

5. **Febold's strange animal was a:**
   a. teddy bear
   b. huggy bear
   c. huggag ✓

6. **A coyote is:**
   a. a river
   b. a wild, dog-like animal ✓
   c. an elephant

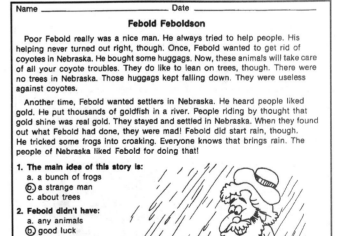

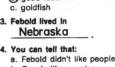

**Brainwork!** Think about the question. Answer it on the back. Draw a picture of what you think a huggag looks like.

Page 76

# Answer Key

Name _____ Date _____

## Pecos Bill

Pecos Bill was a western hero. He was, in fact, the most famous man in the country. Bill invented roping. Bill used to rope everything around. He'd lasso the buzzards and eagles in the sky. He pulled them right down to the ground. Pecos Bill roped bears, wolves, elk and buffalo. He thought a train was a strange kind of animal. He roped it and almost wrecked it, too. Bill's horse was as tough as Bill. He ate barbed wire. That made him tough and mean. Once, Pecos Bill made a bet. He said he could ride a cyclone. He lassoed it over Kansas. That cyclone couldn't throw Bill off. Finally, it gave up and just turned into rain. Pecos Bill had the biggest ranch in the west. He needed water for his cattle. Bill dug the Rio Grande. He filled it with water from the Gulf of Mexico.

1. **The main idea of this story is:**
   a. about horses
   b. about rain
   c. about a western hero
2. **Pecos Bill liked to use:**
   a. his spurs
   b. his rope
   c. big saddles
3. **Pecos Bill dug**
   **the Rio Grande** .
4. **You can tell that:**
   a. Bill was an unusual man.
   b. Bill was afraid of horses.
   c. Bill knew all about trains.
5. **Bill lassoed the cyclone over:**
   a. Texas
   b. Kansas
   c. Arizona
6. **A cyclone is:**
   a. a big cloud
   b. a snowstorm
   c. a big wind

**Brainwork!** Think about the question. Answer it on the back. What would be useful about being a champion roper?

Page 77

---

Name _____ Date _____

## Kemp Morgan

Kemp Morgan was quite a man! He was, in fact, the most famous man in Oklahoma. He was, in fact, the man who discovered oil! In Kemp's oilfields, there was no crew. Kemp was the only worker. He could do everything himself. Kemp found oil this way: he'd walk around the fields. He'd keep his nose near the ground. Sometimes Kemp would stop. He'd sniff and sniff. He'd know by the smell if there was oil below. Kemp would dig for oil. He was always right. Often, Kemp would buy the land with the oil smell. Sometimes he'd give it away to others. Kemp just liked to smell oil for fun. When Kemp would dig a well he'd start with a shovel. Then he'd shoot the hole even bigger with his gun. He'd drill for the oil himself. Finally, he'd build tanks for the oil and put a cap on the well.

1. **The main idea of this story is:**
   a. an oily smell
   b. a man who loved oil
   c. drilling for water
2. **Sometimes Kemp would:**
   a. ask others to help him
   b. keep the land for himself
   c. get a cold
3. **Kemp kept his nose**
   **near the ground** .
4. **You can guess that:**
   a. Kemp knew a lot about oil.
   b. Kemp had a bad sense of smell.
   c. Oil has no smell.
5. **Kemp was famous in:**
   a. New York
   b. Alaska
   c. Oklahoma
6. **A crew is:**
   a. an oil well
   b. a big tank
   c. a group of people working together

**Brainwork!** Think about the question. Answer it on the back. What are your favorite things to smell? Make a list of them.

Page 78

---

Name _____ Date _____

## A.B. Stormalong

He sure was tall! Stormalong stood thirty feet tall, in fact. He signed on as a sailor on the Lady of the Sea. The captain was glad to have such a giant on board. Old Stormalong's size and strength helped him on the sea. He didn't have to climb to set the sails. He'd just reach up high and do it. Stormalong ate too much, though. For lunch he liked a rowboat full of soup. Once, the crew couldn't get the ship started. Old Stormy jumped overboard to have a look. Then he disappeared. Soon, the crew saw a huge, black octopus arm in the air. They were all mighty scared. No man could fight a thing like that! But, suddenly, Old Stormalong climbed back on board! He wasn't even hurt! "Wow!" he sighed. "That old octopus had one hundred arms! Fifty of them were trying to hold the boat down. The others were trying to hold me down! I fixed him, though. I tied every one of those arms in a double knot." Everyone cheered.

1. **The main idea of this story is:**
   a. some small fish
   b. jumping overboard
   c. a great sailor
2. **After the fight, Stormalong:**
   a. got back on the ship
   b. sank to the bottom
   c. made friends with the octopus
3. **Stormy tied the octopus' arms**
   **in double knots** .
4. **You can tell that Stormy was:**
   a. afraid of fish
   b. very brave
   c. short
5. **How many arms did the octopus have?**
   a. none
   b. one hundred
   c. fifty
6. **An octopus is really:**
   a. a sea creature with eight arms
   b. a fish with many fins
   c. a kind of shark

**Brainwork!** Think about the question. Answer it on the back. Why did Stormalong say that the octopus had so many arms?

Page 79

---

Name _____ Date _____

## Finn MacCool

Old Man Mazuma had a problem. He wanted water to go into the desert. That way, plants could bloom. Mazuma lived near the river between the United States and Mexico. It is called the Rio Grande. "Let me think," said Mazuma. "I need the world's greatest engineer." Mazuma talked to lots of folks. They all said that the man he needed was Finn MacCool. Finn was the biggest man Mazuma had ever seen. He could leap over a hill in just one leap! Finn had even built the Great Wall of China, people said. Finn carefully made his plans. He hired Irish and Chinese workers. Finn and his men dug a huge ditch. The Colorado River started to run through it. Finn was so pleased with his work. He smiled and said, "What a Grand Canyon!" And that's what it's called to this day!

1. **The main idea of this story is:**
   a. the Great Wall of China
   b. the greatest engineer
   c. a river in Mexico
2. **Old Man Mazuma needed:**
   a. water in the desert
   b. a shovel
   c. a Chinese worker
3. **Finn called his ditch**
   **a Grand Canyon** .
4. **You can tell that:**
   a. Finn didn't like Mazuma.
   b. Finn liked his work.
   c. Finn was tiny.
5. **How did Finn get over a hill?**
   a. He drove a car.
   b. He flew over it.
   c. He leaped over in one leap.
6. **An engineer is:**
   a. someone who plants seeds
   b. someone who runs over hills
   c. someone who plans and builds things

**Brainwork!** Think about the question. Answer it on the back. Do you think Finn really made the Grand Canyon? Why or why not?

Page 80

# Answer Key

## Page 83 — Tony Beaver

Name _____ Date _____

**Tony Beaver**

Tony was the most famous logger in the South. He did everything in a big way. Once, Tony decided to grow peanuts. (He called them goobers.) Well, Tony just grew too many goobers. That year, his maple trees had too much sap, too. So, Tony was stuck with molasses from the maple sap. It started to rain. Tony's town was flooded. Tony's neighbors asked him to stop the flood. Tony and his friends took the goobers out of their shells. They dumped them into the overflowing Eel River. Next, they dumped in the molasses. The sun came out. It was so hot that the river started boiling. The smell coming from the river made everyone hungry. Tony began mixing the goobers, molasses, and river. He stirred for hours. Tony cooled the river. The mixture hardened. Tony took it out. He broke it into pieces. Everyone in town wanted to taste it. It was great! Tony had saved the town. He had also invented peanut brittle!

1. The main idea of this story is:
   a. a hero and inventor
   b. about sap
   c. a boiling river

2. Tony's neighbors knew:
   a. He didn't like goobers.
   b. He could help them.
   c. He couldn't swim.

3. What did Tony invent?
   Tony invented peanut brittle.

4. You can tell that:
   a. Tony's town was big.
   b. Tony couldn't help anyone.
   c. Tony was very smart.

5. The river started boiling when:
   a. The sun came out.
   b. Tony cut down some trees.
   c. The weather got cold.

6. Sap is:
   a. boiling river water
   b. a sticky liquid in trees
   c. a flood

**Brainwork!** Think about the question. Answer it on the back. Tell what you think peanut brittle tastes like.

## Page 82 — Paul Bunyan and Babe Go West

Name _____ Date _____

**Paul Bunyan and Babe Go West**

Paul Bunyan had cleared all the land of North Dakota. He planted a seed of corn. It grew way up into the sky. Paul's friend Ole climbed it. His head disappeared into the clouds. Suddenly Ole shouted, "Paul! From up here I see a big ocean! I see a great land of big trees." Ole had seen the Pacific. Paul decided that he and Babe should go west. On the long trip, Babe got thirsty. Paul dug a well. Was he surprised! Boiling hot water gushed out of the well. Paul saw that it did every hour. "I'll call it Old Faithful," he said. You can still see Old Faithful in Yellowstone Park today. Paul kept going and finally reached Washington. The trees were ready for cutting. Then he'd send the logs from China. So Paul had to dig out a river that went straight to the Pacific Ocean. He called it the Columbia River. Those logs sailed right over to China! Paul Bunyan sure was the biggest, strongest man that ever lived!

1. The main idea of this story is:
   a. trees from China
   b. digging a well
   c. a great logger

2. Paul wanted to go west to:
   a. sail to China
   b. cut trees
   c. plant corn

3. Paul's friend Ole saw
   an ocean and big trees.

4. You can tell that:
   a. Paul didn't like to travel.
   b. Paul liked Babe.
   c. Paul was a farmer.

5. Paul called the well:
   a. Old Well
   b. Old Yellowstone
   c. Old Faithful

6. A logger:
   a. cuts trees down
   b. sits on logs all the time
   c. helps beavers cut logs

**Brainwork!** Think about the question. Answer it on the back. What could you see from the top of a giant corn plant?

## Page 86 — Dinosaur Words

Name _____ Skill: Dictionary

**Dinosaur Words**

These words will teach you more about dinosaurs. Look up the words in your dictionary. Write each definition on the lines. Keep this page in your desk. It will help you remember the words when you are doing other pages in this book.

1. fossil: The remains or traces of an animal or plant that lived long ago.

2. reptile: A cold-blooded animal that has a backbone.

3. prehistoric: Belonging to a time before people started writing history.

4. extinct: No longer existing.

5. dinosaur: One of a large group of extinct reptiles that lived millions of years ago.

Look up the underlined words in your dictionary. Then complete the sentences.

6. Tyrannosaurus Rex was the largest carnivore. It ate: meat

7. Animals with vertebrate have: backbones

## Page 85 — Iguanodon

Name _____ Skill: Multiple Comprehension

**Iguanodon** Pronunciation: ig-WAN-o-don

It was a warm spring day in 1822. While walking down a hill, Mary Mantell noticed a strange looking rock. "These look like teeth," Mary said. Mary showed the rock to her husband. He was a paleontologist, a person who studies fossils and ancient life forms.

"These are fossils," stated Dr. Mantell. "They look like the teeth of a giant iguana lizard. This is an amazing discovery! Let's see if we can find more fossils." In time, the Mantells found many giant-sized bones. They put the bones together like a puzzle. The giant creature was called Iguanodon.

During the 1800s, thousands more fossils were found throughout the world. These creatures came to be called dinosaurs, which means "terrible lizards."

1. A good title for this story is:
   a. Digging Up Rocks
   b. The Discovery of Giant Bones
   c. How Fossil Teeth Look

2. What did Mary Mantell discover?
   Mary discovered fossils.

3. Dinosaurs were called "terrible lizards" because:
   a. They crawled on the ground.
   b. They had long tails.
   c. They looked like giant monsters.

4. How did Dr. Mantell feel about Mary's discovery?
   Dr. Mantell felt it was an amazing discovery.

**Brainwork!** Would you like to spend one year digging for dinosaur bones in the desert? Tell why or why not.

## Page 81 — Captain Kidd

Name _____ Date _____

**Captain Kidd**

Long ago, there were pirates along the eastern coast of America. Captain Kidd was a sailor from New York. He said he'd sail off and catch some pirates. When Captain Kidd found the pirates, he was surprised. They seemed to be having so much fun! Captain Kidd said to himself, "I think I'll become a pirate, too. But I'll keep it a secret." When Captain Kidd wanted to go back to New York, though, he couldn't. Everybody knew that he'd become a pirate. The king's soldiers were after him. The captain kept robbing ships. He had stolen lots of gold and jewels. Finally, the soldiers caught up with him. Captain Kidd was killed. People knew he had hidden his treasures. They were buried in New York and New Jersey. Captain Kidd had sent terrible, ugly ghosts to guard the treasures. People don't give up easily, though. The treasures of Captain Kidd are still buried somewhere. If you find one, be careful of those ghosts!

1. The main idea of this story is:
   a. the king's soldiers
   b. a pirate and his treasure
   c. sailing a ship

2. Captain Kidd thought that:
   a. The life of a pirate looked great.
   b. Pirates wore dirty clothes.
   c. He didn't like gold.

3. Captain Kidd's treasure is guarded by ghosts.

4. You can tell that Captain Kidd:
   a. still sails the sea
   b. didn't want you to have his treasure
   c. gave his treasure away

5. Captain Kidd's treasure is in:
   a. California
   b. North and South Dakota
   c. New York and New Jersey

6. Treasure is:
   a. junk
   b. something that's worth a lot
   c. only gold

**Brainwork!** Think about the question. Answer it on the back. Why do you think Captain Kidd doesn't want anyone to have his treasure?

## Page 84 — John Darling

Name _____ Date _____

**John Darling**

When John was a little boy, there was nothing special about him. But when he got older, he chopped down a tree. He even split the stump of the tree. Was John surprised! The stump grew together again after he'd split it! John thought it was magic. He knew it meant he'd be a great man. John went to work on the Erie Canal. He had a fine boat. John wanted to marry a girl named Sal. Sal said she'd marry the man who caught the most fish. John's friends were catching lots of fish. John didn't even have one. Suddenly, he had an idea. Sal was with him on the boat. She had the reddest, shiniest hair. John told her to lean her head over the side. She did. The fish liked the light from Sal's hair. They jumped right into the boat! Soon, John Darling had a boat full of fish. A while later, he also had a wife named Sal.

1. The main idea of this story is:
   a. catching fish
   b. a boatman on the Erie Canal
   c. building a canal

2. John knew that:
   a. Someday he'd be important.
   b. Sal didn't like fish.
   c. He'd never marry Sal.

3. Why did the fish jump into the boat?
   They liked the light from Sal's hair.

4. You can guess that:
   a. John couldn't chop trees down.
   b. Sal got seasick.
   c. Sal thought John was a smart man.

5. What kind of hair did Sal have?
   a. blond and curly
   b. red and shiny
   c. black and short

6. A stump of a tree is:
   a. the part that's left after cutting
   b. a bunch of leaves
   c. a branch

**Brainwork!** Think about the question. Answer it on the back. Why do you think this story is true or not true?

125

# Answer Key

## Page 89

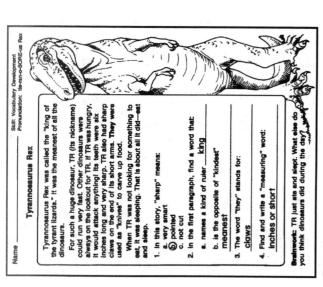

Name _____

Skill: Vocabulary Development
Pronunciation: tie-ran-o-SORE-us Rex

### Tyrannosaurus Rex

Tyrannosaurus Rex was called the "king of the tyrant lizards." It was the meanest of all the dinosaurs.

For such a huge dinosaur, TR (its nickname) could run very fast. Other dinosaurs were always on the lookout for TR. If TR was hungry, it would attack anything! Its teeth were six inches long and very sharp. TR also had sharp claws on the end of its short arms. They were used as "knives" to carve up food.

When TR was not looking for something to eat, it was sleeping. That is about all it did—eat and sleep.

1. In this story, "sharp" means:
   a. very smart
   b. pointed
   c. not cut

2. In the first paragraph, find a word that:
   a. names a kind of ruler __king__
   b. is the opposite of "kindest" __meanest__

3. The word "they" stands for:
   __claws__

4. Find and write a "measuring" word:
   __inches or short__

**Brainwork:** TR just ate and slept. What else do you think dinosaurs did during the day? _____

Page 89

## Page 92

Name _____

Skill: Recalling Information
Pronunciation: ter-o-DAK-til-us

### Pterodactylus

Read the story carefully. After 90 seconds, turn the paper over and answer the questions. Do not look back.

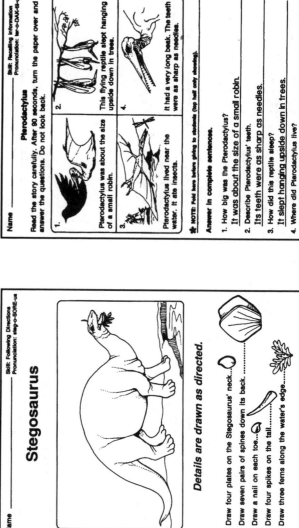

1.
2. This flying reptile slept hanging upside down in trees.
Pterodactylus was about the size of a small robin.
It had a very long beak. The teeth were as sharp as needles.
3.
4.
Pterodactylus lived near the water. It ate insects.

✱ NOTE: Fold here before giving to students (top half only showing).

Answer in complete sentences.

1. How big was the Pterodactylus?
   __It was about the size of a small robin.__

2. Describe Pterodactylus' teeth.
   __Its teeth were as sharp as needles.__

3. How did this reptile sleep?
   __It slept hanging upside down in trees.__

4. Where did Pterodactylus live?
   __It lived near the water.__

Page 92

## Page 88

Name _____

Skill: Sequencing
Pronunciation: bruck-ee-o-SORE-us

### Brachiosaurus

Read the first sentence in each box. Decide what comes next. Find the correct sentence ending in the water below the Brachiosaurus and write it.

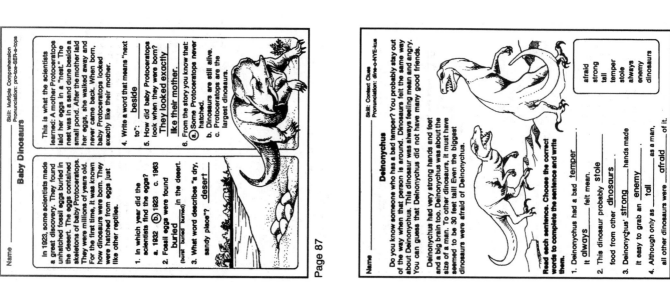

1. Brachiosaurus was the biggest of the big. It measured 85 feet
   __from head to toe__

2. Brachiosaurus moved very slowly. It stayed in water, safe
   __from unfriendly dinosaurs__

3. This dinosaur weighed about 80 tons, which is as much as
   __16 large elephants weigh__

from head to toe
from unfriendly dinosaurs
run away too fast
a bird weighs
16 large elephants weigh

**Brainwork:** Write three things you could do much better if your neck was as long as Brachiosaurus'.

Page 88

## Page 91

Name _____

Skill: Following Directions
Pronunciation: stego-o-SORE-us

### Stegosaurus

*Details are drawn as directed.*

1. Draw four plates on the Stegosaurus' neck. ........
2. Draw seven pairs of spines down its back. ........
3. Draw a nail on each toe. ........
4. Draw four spikes on the tail. ........
5. Draw three ferns along the water's edge. ........

Page 91

## Page 87

Name _____

Skill: Multiple Comprehension
Pronunciation: pro-toe-SER-a-tops

### Baby Dinosaurs

In 1923, some scientists made a great discovery. They found unhatched fossil eggs buried in the desert. The eggs contained skeletons of baby Protoceratops. They were millions of years old. For the first time, it was known how dinosaurs were born. They were hatched from eggs just like other reptiles.

This is what the scientists learned: A mother Protoceratops laid her eggs in a "nest." The nest was in a sand dune beside a small pond. After the mother laid her eggs, she walked away and never came back. When born, baby Protoceratops looked exactly like their mother.

1. In which year did the scientists find the eggs?
   a. 1932   b. 1923   c. 1953

2. Fossil eggs were found __buried__ in the desert.
   (burst buried buried)

3. What word describes "a dry, sandy place"? __desert__

4. Write a word that means "next to":
   __beside__

5. How did baby Protoceratops look when they were born?
   __They looked exactly like their mother.__

6. From the story you know that:
   a. Some Protoceratops never hatched.
   b. Dinosaurs are still alive.
   c. Protoceratops are the largest dinosaurs.

Page 87

## Page 90

Name _____

Skill: Context Clues
Pronunciation: dine-o-NYE-kus

### Deinonychus

Do you know someone who has a bad temper? You probably stay out of the way when that person is around. Dinosaurs felt the same way about Deinonychus. This dinosaur was always feeling mean and angry. You can guess that Deinonychus did not have many good friends.

Deinonychus had very strong hands and feet and a big brain too. To other dinosaurs, it must have seemed to be 30 feet tall. Even the biggest dinosaurs were afraid of Deinonychus.

afraid
strong
tall
temper
stole
always
enemy
dinosaurs

Read each sentence. Choose the correct words to complete the sentence and write them.

1. Deinonychus had a bad __temper__.
   It __always__ felt mean.

2. This dinosaur probably __stole__ food from other __dinosaurs__.

3. Deinonychus' __strong__ hands made it easy to grab an __enemy__.

4. Although only as __tall__ as a man, all other dinosaurs were __afraid__ of it.

Page 90

FS-32044 Reading

# Answer Key

## Page 93 — Elephant Bird

**Skill: Sentence Completion**

The elephant bird was one of the largest birds ever to live. It was about eleven feet tall. Even though this bird had feathers, it could not fly.

Scientists have found huge fossil elephant bird eggshells. One shell could hold two gallons! Can you imagine eating an egg that big for breakfast?

There are many legends about the elephant bird. One story says that the bird could pick up an elephant in its claws and carry it away. (I thought the elephant bird couldn't fly, didn't you?)

**What comes before? What comes after? Complete each sentence. Read the story for clues.**

1. The elephant bird could not fly even though __it had__ feathers.

2. One shell could hold two gallons. __Could you__ eat an egg that big?

3. The elephant bird, one of the largest birds, was about __eleven__ feet tall.

4. A __legend__ is a story that is not always true.

## Page 94 — Archaeopteryx

**Skill: Context Clues**
**Pronunciation: ar-kay-OP-tur-iks**

The next time you see a bird, look at it very carefully. Did you know that it is a real living relative of the dinosaur? Archaeopteryx is the first known bird that ever lived. It looked just like a small dinosaur except for one thing: feathers. This early bird was about the size of a crow. Most birds can fly, but the Archaeopteryx could not. It walked around on rocks or in tree branches.

Archaeopteryx was the first bird. Do you think birds will ever grow into huge dinosaurs like Tyrannosaurus Rex again? Tell why or why not. Write your answer on the back.

**Read each sentence. Choose the correct word from the box and write it.**

first
crow
Earth
feathers
footprints
could
small
because

1. Archaeopteryx looked like a __small__ dinosaur with __feathers__.

2. Scientists know Archaeopteryx could walk __because__ they found its __footprints__.

3. Archaeopteryx was about the size of a __crow__ although it __could__ not fly.

4. Archaeopteryx was the __first__ bird ever to live on __Earth__.

## Page 95 — Elasmosaurus

**Skill: Comprehension**
**Pronunciation: ee-laz-mo-SORE-us**

Elasmosaurus looked like a giant floating turtle. It would paddle along on top of the water looking for things to eat. Elasmosaurus was not a picky eater. It took a lot of food to fill up its huge stomach.

This dinosaur could not swim very fast, but that didn't matter. It had such a long neck, it could easily snatch a fish swimming 20 feet away. Elasmosaurus used its flippers as oars to paddle around the ocean. Some scientists think this sea monster could "row" backwards as well as forwards.

1. What did Elasmosaurus look like? __It looked like a giant floating turtle.__

2. Find a sentence in the story that means the same as: "Elasmosaurus didn't have a favorite food." __Elasmosaurus was not a picky eater.__

3. Elasmosaurus could catch a fish swimming __20__ feet away.

4. Find a word that is the opposite of "let go." __snatch__

5. Another giant sea monster could easily catch Elasmosaurus. __True__ False
Tell why or why not. Write your answer on the back.

## Page 96 — Tylosaurus

**Skill: Locating Facts**
**Pronunciation: tile-o-SORE-us**

If you had gone deep sea diving 70 million years ago, guess what would have been down there with you! A Tylosaurus, that's what. This dinosaur looked like a crocodile, but it was as big as a great white shark! Its huge jaw and sharp teeth made it look even more fierce—especially when it was hungry!

A long powerful tail helped the Tylosaurus swim at fast speeds. A slower moving sea monster would have had a hard time escaping the bite of the Tylosaurus. Can you imagine a fight between a Tylosaurus and an Elasmosaurus? The whipping and thrashing of tails would make it seem like a hurricane.

**Answer the questions in complete sentences.**

1. What made the Tylosaurus look so fierce? __Its huge jaw and sharp teeth made it look fierce.__

2. How long ago did the Tylosaurus live? __It lived 70 million years ago.__

3. Why was the Tylosaurus so fast? __It had a long powerful tail that helped it swim fast.__

4. What would a Tylosaurus and Elasmosaurus fight seem like? __It would seem like a hurricane.__

5. On the back, draw and color a sea monster that looks like: a whale, a lizard and a dolphin.

## Page 97 — Dinohyus

**Skill: Reading Comprehension**
**Pronunciation: DY-no-hy-us**

Dinohyus was a strange-looking mammal that lived about 40 million years ago. It had split hooves and two strong tusks just like pigs of today do. Large bones stuck out around the eyes. To make matters worse, its face looked like a baboon. When scientists found Dinohyus skeletons, they noticed that many had broken bones. They probably broke their bones fighting enemies—and losing!

1. What happened to the dinosaurs? __The dinosaurs became extinct.__

2. Name 3 kinds of mammals. __Answers will vary.__

3. Find another word for "climate." Write it on the line. __weather__

4. When did Dinohyus live? __They lived about 40 million years ago.__

5. How did Dinohyus' face look? __Its face looked like a baboon.__

6. In what way did Dinohyus look like a pig? __It had split hooves and two strong tusks.__

## Page 98 — Ankylosaurus

**Skill: Comprehension**
**Pronunciation: an-kill-o-SORE-us**

Ankylosaurus looked like a "crawling tank." Its head and back were covered with plates of armor. Even the tail had heavy bones in it. The Ankylosaurus used its tail as a club. If an enemy got too close, Ankylosaurus would knock it flat. What a headache! Ankylosaurus had very tiny teeth and probably ate only soft plants.

**Answer the questions in complete sentences.**

1. How did Ankylosaurus use its tail? __It used its tail as a club.__

2. What did Ankylosaurus eat? __It ate only soft plants.__

3. What did an Ankylosaurus look like? __It looked like a "crawling tank."__

4. What protected the Ankylosaurus' head? __Plates of armor covered its head.__

Draw the Ankylosaurus. Give it something to eat.

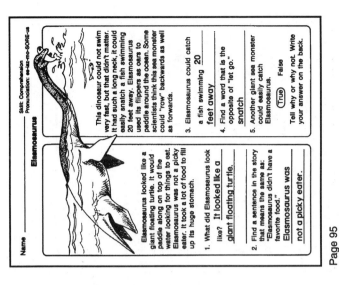

FS-32044 Reading

# Answer Key

---

**Name** — Skill: Identification

## Dinosaur Tales

Read the clues about each dinosaur. Find the correct matching picture. Write the dinosaur's name on the line.

a. _____ Tyrannosaurus Rex
b. _____ Triceratops
c. _____ Ankylosaurus
d. _____ Diplodocus
e. _____ Corythosaurus

1. **Triceratops**—It had three horns on its head. Its mouth was shaped like a beak.

2. **Corythosaurus**—This dinosaur had a head shaped like a helmet. Its "hands" were webbed like the feet of a duck.

3. **Diplodocus**—This was the longest dinosaur. It was 90 feet from head to tail.

4. **Tyrannosaurus Rex** was a very fierce dinosaur. Its teeth were six inches long! Its arms were very short.

5. **Ankylosaurus**—This dinosaur looked like a "walking tank." Its tail looked like a club.

Page 101

---

**Name** — Skill: Sequencing

## Make a Fossil!

Making your own fossil is easy and fun. All you need is plaster of Paris, clay, a narrow piece of tagboard and a leaf (or shell).

1.

2. Make a ring out of the tagboard and press it into the clay. Press the leaf into the clay. Make it lie flat.

3. Flatten the clay (¾" thickness) into a circle larger than the leaf.

4. When the plaster has hardened, remove the ring and peel away the clay. Peel the leaf off—gently! Now you have a fossil!

Mix plaster of Paris with water until it turns to a thin paste. Pour over the leaf (about ½") and let it set.

**Write these sentences in order as they happened in the story.**

_____ Peel off the leaf.                    1. Flatten the clay.
_____ Press leaf into the clay.             2. Press leaf into the clay.
_____ Flatten the clay.                     3. Mix plaster of Paris.
_____ Mix plaster of Paris.                 4. Peel off the leaf.

Page 104

---

**Name** — Skill: Multiple Comprehension
Pronunciation: bron-toe-SORE-us

## Brontosaurus

The first human had not yet been born 65 million years ago. How then do we know that dinosaurs really existed? Read the story under each picture to find out.

1. 130 million years ago...

2. Its skin rots. The bones are covered with dirt carried by the wind.

3. The Brontosaurus dies in the forest.

4. Thousands of years later, the dirt and bones turn into stone.

5. Heavy rains beat against the mountain. The rock wears away.

6. 100 years ago... Brontosaurus remains hidden for millions of years.

A scientist finds Brontosaurus' bones. These bones are called fossils.

1. Write a word that means the same as "rock." **stone**

2. The Brontosaurus was hidden for **millions** of years.
   It was buried under a **mountain**.

3. Fact or Opinion? The scientist was very excited when he discovered the fossils. **Opinion**

**Brainwork:** What do you think animals will look like in 30 million years? Write three sentences on the back. Draw a picture.

Page 100

---

**Name** — Skill: Understanding Sentences

## Finding Fossils

Let's go on a fossil hunt. Cut out the sentences. Look at each picture carefully. Decide which sentence best fits this picture. Paste it in the box.

1. c. All ready. These fossils are ready to go to the museum.

2. f. Let's put up a tent and start looking for more bones.

3. a. I'll put a number on all these bones before packing them.

4. e. Wow! This dinosaur was huge. Take pictures.

5. d. Be careful! It's easy to shatter those bones.

6. b. Look! I think I've found a fossil.

a. I'll put a number on all these bones before packing them.
b. Look! I think I've found a fossil.
c. All ready. These fossils are ready to go to the museum.
d. Be careful! It's easy to shatter those bones.
e. Wow! This dinosaur was huge. Take pictures.
f. Let's put up a tent and start looking for more bones.

Page 103

---

**Name** — Skill: Multiple Comprehension
Pronunciation: AN-tee-ark

## Antiarch

Antiarch looked like a swimming submarine. It lived 350 million years ago in fresh water streams. Most of the Antiarch's body did not have scales. However, armor did cover its head and a part of its back.

Do you see two strange looking "claws" near the Antiarch's head? This fish swam close to the bottom of a stream. Maybe the claws helped push Antiarch through plants and rocks. Antiarch ate small fish. How do you think it swallowed its food? Draw a picture on the back showing what Antiarch looked like without its face armor.

1. A good title for this story is:
   a. The Story of Armor
   b. A Strange Prehistoric Fish
   c. How Antiarch Swam

2. How long ago did Antiarch live?
   **It lived 350 million years ago.**

3. Where did Antiarch swim?
   **It swam close to the bottom of a stream.**

4. What did Antiarch look like?
   **It looked like a swimming submarine.**

5. "Scales" protect a fish. Write a different meaning for the word "scales."
   **Answers vary.**

**Brainwork:** Think of two reasons why Antiarch had those "claws." Answer in a complete sentence. **Answers vary.**

Page 99

---

**Name** — Skill: Multiple Comprehension

## Where Did They Go?

What ever happened to the dinosaurs? About 65 million years ago, they became extinct. Scientists are not sure, but they think perhaps:

a) A huge star crashed into Earth, making it as hot as an oven. The heat may have killed the plants that dinosaurs ate.

b) Dinosaurs could live only in a warm climate. Over the years, the weather cooled down. Dinosaurs could not keep warm. Can you imagine a Brontosaurus trying to curl up in a cave? Dinosaurs ruled the earth for about 140 million years. Scientists are still finding their fossils. Who knows what other amazing secrets may still be hidden beneath the earth?

1. What may have killed the plants?
   Heat from a huge star may have killed the plants.

2. How did the weather change?
   The weather cooled down.

3. When did dinosaurs become extinct?
   Dinosaurs became extinct about 65 million years ago.

4. What word means the same as "died out"?
   extinct

5. Why couldn't dinosaurs live in cold weather?
   They could not keep warm.

**Brainwork:** Pretend you have a pet dinosaur. What would you do to keep it warm in winter?

Page 102

---

128